Our Message is Christ

Our Message is Christ

THE MORE OUTSTANDING ELEMENTS
OF THE CHRISTIAN MESSAGE

JOHANNES HOFINGER, SJ

Fides Publishers
Notre Dame, Indiana

Notre Dame, Indiana 46556
With permission of the Superiors.
Nihil Obstat: Lawrence A. Gollner
Censor Librorum
Imprimatur: Leo A. Pursley, D.D.
Bishop of Ft. Wayne—South Bend

ISBN: 0-8190-0498-7

Preface

After Vatican Council II there has been much confusion about what Catholics really do believe and should believe, and how it all fits together. Investigations of theologians have raised more questions than provided answers. What is needed is a clear, balanced presentation of the central truths of Christian faith in such a way that they nourish Christian life.

The National Conference of Catholic Bishops has tried to meet this need with the booklet, *Basic Teachings for Catholic Religious Education*, which is an expanded version of part of the *General Catechetical Directory*. Father Johannes Hofinger, the great apostle of kerygmatic renewal, has provided a much fuller presentation, which would be most helpful to religious educators, to parents, and to many of the clergy as well. *Our Message is Christ* can be used for meditative reading, for homilies, for adult education lecture series, and as background for discussion groups. The questions at the beginning and end of each session should be particularly valuable in opening up discussion.

The great advantage of Father Hofinger's treatment is that in brief, almost outline form he shows how doctrines nourish faith and why they are *good news* to Christians. His analysis springs from prayer and leads to prayer. His aim is not simply understanding but the kind of understanding of God's revelation which deepens and enriches the life of faith.

It has been a joy and a privilege for me to work with Father Hofinger on several projects. His boundless energy and enthusiasm in proclaiming the message of Christ radiates through these pages. Would that all who read this book might be enkindled with his spark!

Francis J. Buckley, S.J.

University of San Francisco
Easter, 1973

Contents

Introduction

Human nutrition means definitely more than providing the human body with the necessary quantity of water, protein and carbohydrate. But the new emphasis of vitamins and other important nutrients does not mean that we can now nourish the human body quite well without providing it the necessary quantity of water, protein and carbohydrate. In the same way Christian education requires definitely more than just present-Christian doctrine. But does that mean that we can now form true Christians without acquainting them, according to their age and capacity, with God's plan for their lives, without presenting to them the truth of God's loving concern for man which gives their lives its true meaning?

It is a sign of hope that countless religion teachers—priests, sisters and laymen alike—are again aware that religious education without solid doctrinal substance leads to nothing. But with this new awareness let us not fall back on the old overemphasis on a multitude of particular doctrines, showing a greater concern for the intellectual aspect of Christian education than for a living faith. The emphasis must be put on Christian life, guided and motivated by an ever deeper and more inspiring insight into God's loving plan for man's life and fulfillment.

The present book takes its subtitle from the third part of the *General Catechetical Directory* which deals with "the more outstanding elements of the Christian message". Thus the book presents itself as some aid in attaining the purpose of the *Directory*. In its excellent chapter on the "Norms and Criteria" with regard to the content of religious instruction, the Roman document rightly insists that the Christian message must be presented as an organic unity. "A catechesis which neglects this inter-relation and harmony of its content can become entirely useless for achieving its proper end" (GCD, n.39). However, in presenting "the more outstanding elements of the Christian message" (nn.47-69) the authors of the *Directory* deliberately dispense with making "an attempt to show a suitable way for ordering the truths of faith according to an organic plan in a kind of synthesis" (n.36). But this is exactly what the priests and catechists need for their work in order to integrate all the particular doctrines impressively into the one gospel of God's saving love.

It is the special aim of the present book to serve all who teach religion by presenting the more important elements of the Christian message in the light of Christ who is the very center of all. Throughout the whole book the reader will notice the continuous endeavor to make the Roman guidelines fruitful for a timely teaching of religion in family, school and church.

The author is deeply indebted to his friends Sister Maria de la Cruz, H.H.S. and Father Francis Buckley, S.J., in San Francisco, as well as to Sister Paula Richard, O.P., in New Orleans, for their generous help in editing the text and enriching it considerably with their many suggestions.

Abbreviations

GCD	General Catechetical Directory
CR	Constitution on Divine Revelation
CCH	Dogmatic Constitution on the Church
CMW	Pastoral Constitution on the Church in the Modern World
CL	Constitution on Sacred Liturgy
CM	Degree on the Missionary Activity of the Church
DAL	Decree on the Apostolate of the Laity

1

Our Aim

What does it mean to be a catechist? What is his real task? How to evaluate the result of our catechetical efforts?

Whoever works in the ministry of the word—catechist and preacher alike—is the witness and spokesman of God. It is his privilege to serve God as a free instrument in His communication with man. He cannot serve well without having a clear idea of what God aims at in speaking to man. Even more, in his whole work he must make God's loving intention his very own.

1. God's aim

"In His goodness and wisdom, God chose to reveal Himself and to make known to us the hidden purpose of His will (cf. Eph 1:9), by which through Christ, the Word made flesh, man has access to the Father in the Holy Spirit and comes to share in the divine nature (cf. Eph 2:18; 2 Pt 1:4). Through this revelation, therefore, the invisible God (cf. Col 1:15; 1 Tm 1:17) out of the abundance of His love speaks to men as friends (cf. Ex 33:11; Jn 15:14-15) and lives among them (cf. Ba 3:38), so that He may invite and take them into fellowship with Himself" (CR, n. 2).

In order to correct less appropriate formulations, Vatican II stresses (with this fundamental text) the "abundance of His love" as the main motive of God's revelation. He intends to *establish a true friendship with man*. This, therefore, has to be the aim of all catechetical efforts: To lead those to be catechized, according to their age and particular condition, step by step to a friendship which God Himself wishes to establish with each person and with the whole Christian community. In preconciliar catechesis the emphasis was quite often on memorization of a particular catechism or on "learning" of Christian religion. Renewed catechesis, too, to be sure, engages the memory and even more the intellect, but it sees memorization and even the intellectual assimilation of the Christian message only as means to be used to achieve the aim of all catechesis: To lead to a relationship of true love with God which grows ever more deep and committed, i.e., to a life of ever more perfect friendship with God. Therefore the decisive criterion of successful catechesis does not consist in what those to be catechized know at the end of the catechetical instruction, but in the efficient help they have received for a truly Christian life which by its very nature is a life of love. It goes without saying that the Christian life cannot grow deep and mature without corresponding intellectual deepening.

2. Some important consequences

According to the Council, God speaks in His revelation to men as friends in order to invite them to a friendship with Him which gives to the life of man its very meaning and fulfillment. Like any communication which aims at friendship, the main motive of God's revelation is love. This is what the Council stresses deliberately in order to correct the false trend of an antiquated theology which, in speaking on God's revelation, emphasized above all God's authority. There is of course no doubt that God, in speaking to us, uses His authority and demands the submission of man in acceptance of His revelation, as the Council itself explicitly stated (CR, n. 5). None the less, in presenting God's revelation correctly, *the main emphasis must be put upon God's love* (See about this also the GCD, n. 10). The catechist must understand himself, above all, as a messenger of God's love. His whole approach and his whole personality must express this impressively. This implies necessarily a deep understanding and true love for the people of here and now to whom God sends him.

Speaking to men as friends, God intends his revelation to do essentially more than to inform man about things which surpass human horizons, or to provide him with exciting news from another world, or to test his readiness to submit his intellect. When a friend speaks to a friend he wishes to communicate himself to his friend and to express his loving intention. This is, according to Vatican II, exactly the intention of God who wishes "to show forth and communicate Himself and the eternal decisions of His will regarding the salvation of men" (CR, n. 6).

In preconciliar catechesis we met quite often a wrong emphasis upon the particular doctrines of the Christian message. It presented itself too much as a long list of truths which we have to faithfully agree upon in order to prove the submission of our intellect. According to the Council, the emphasis is to be put upon the loving intention of God who manifests Himself. The particular doctrines (Trinity, Incarnation, Church, Sacraments etc.) must be understood and presented as the integral parts of this *selfmanifestation of the Divine Lover* and his personal concern for the well-being of His friend, man.

Friends communicate one with the other by signs. Among these signs, words have great importance, but *deeds* count even more. Preconciliar catechesis, when speaking of divine revelation tended to put more emphasis on verbal revelation and not enough on the revelatory character of the divine deeds. Therefore, the Council insists: "This plan of revelation is realized by deeds and words having an inner unity" (CR, n. 2. See the whole passage). By presenting well what God did and continually does for us in order to prove His loving intention, we convince our brethren best of the love of God.

What counts most in any friendship is *the present*. Friendship is more than the remembrance of a happy past. It is mutual communication of love here and now. Deeds of the past prove only a love of the past. They count in the measure that what they express continues in the present. Especially youngsters of today have no interest in a "history" of salvation which does not distinguish itself by its emphasis on the actual. Any true friendship lives by its actuality and hopes even more in the future. It is for this reason that St. Paul insists that he proclaims "Christ among you, your hope of glory" (Col 1:27).

3. The response God expects

According to Vatican II, revelation does not mean primarily a kind of divine information by which God communicates His ideas in order that we accept them in true submission. It especially means an undeserved invitation by which God challenges man to a true friendship with his Lord God. To this challenge man responds freely, with the help of God, by his faith. *Faith is our thankful and committed YES to God's call.* "The obedience of faith must be given to God who reveals, an obedience by which man entrusts his whole self to God, offering the full submission of intellect and will to God who reveals" (CR, n.5).

By these statements on the nature of faith and on the nature of revelation (CR, n.2), the Council deliberately corrected the overly intellectualistic presentation which generally characterized preconciliar theology. The faith God expects from man as response is essentially more than an intellectual assent to revealed truths. By his faith man not only admits the truth of God's revelation, but freely accepts God's challenge to commit himself to a life of friendship with God. This commitment necessarily includes his readiness for a thorough change of his whole life, i.e., to a true *conversion*.

We encounter here a point of decisive importance for the whole ministry of the word. If revelation means primarily a system of truths, faith obviously consists in the intellectual assent in these truths and catechesis aims, above all, in becoming acquainted with these truths in order that they be assented to. On the contrary, if revelation is by its very nature God's gracious invitation to a new life of friendship with Him, faith consists in the determined acceptance of this invitation and catechesis aims above all at a well considered and truly committed acceptance of this invitation, an acceptance which produces its fruit in life. This is exactly what we mean by *living and mature faith*.

The new emphasis does not, of course, mean a neglect of the intellectual element of catechesis, but only its harmonious integration into the whole process of religious formation.

Following the emphasis of the Council, the new General Catechetical Directory stresses that a living and mature faith, in the sense we just have explained, is the aim of all catechetical activity. The Directory defines catechesis as "that form of ecclesial action which leads both communities and individual members of the faithful to maturity of faith" (GCD, n. 21. See the whole passage). In the following numbers (nn. 21-30) the Directory describes well the qualities of this mature and living faith.

It is obvious then that the catechist, with all his efforts, cannot produce mature faith in others. The catechists "are responsible for choosing and creating suitable conditions which are necessary for the Christian message to be sought, accepted, and more profoundly investigated. This is the point to which the action of catechists extends—and there it stops. For adherence on the part of those to be taught is a fruit of grace and freedom, and does not ultimately depend on the catechist; and catechetical action, therefore, should be accompanied by prayer" (GCD, n. 71).

Mature faith cannot be achieved in the time of childhood, but only much later. The General Catechetical Directory is not afraid of recognizing and even inculcating the necessary consequence: The catechesis of children cannot be considered as catechesis par excellence, but only as an important, yet preparatory stage in the whole process of catechesis. Not catechesis of children, but "*catechesis of adults,* since it deals with persons who are capable of an adherence that is fully responsible, must be considered the chief form of catechesis. All the other forms, which are indeed always necessary, are in some way oriented to it" (GCD, n. 20).

AIDS FOR DISCUSSION AND ASSIMILATION

1. *What is God's main intention in His communication with man? How does the Council express it? Why is this question so important for the catechist?*
2. *What are some of the consequences for the catechetical work if God wants to establish friendship with man?*
3. *What is the main difference between faith according to Vatican II and according to the less precise formulations before the Council?*

God appears there as one who wishes to communicate himself, carrying out a plan which proceeds from love.

Catechesis, then, ought to take its beginning from this gift of divine love. Faith is the acceptance and coming to fruit of the divine gift in us (General Catechetical Directory, n. 10).

2
The Core of Our Message

Have we to present "doctrines" in our catechesis? What is the function of the particular doctrines in authentic catechesis? How to distinguish the more important doctrines from the less important ones?

Because of imprecise ideas about the true meaning and very aim of the ministry of the word, we find in preconciliar catechesis quite often a *lack of the necessary concentration*. Many catechists presented the Christian message as a conglomeration of many particular doctrines without showing very well their coherence, and surely without showing impressively how all the particular doctrines are only the integral parts of one fundamental message. These catechists did not reflect enough about the central idea of the whole Christian revelation and, therefore, they were in want of the necessary criterion for distinguishing correctly the more or less important truths. Hence quite often they spoke more of St. Joseph than of the Holy Spirit, more of Fatima than of the second coming of Christ, more of the Guardian Angel than of divine providence. They may have insisted more on some particular devotions than on the basic attitudes of faith and repentance, and given more importance to the catechism of theologians than to the catechism of God, the Bible.

1. The Second Vatican Council

The Council was aware of the lack of concentration which characterized large sectors of preconciliar catechesis and preaching and tried to remedy it. The Council gave a splendid example by its own presentation of the Christian message. In the Constitution on Revelation it shows lucidly how the whole revelation has its inner unity in Christ in whom God revealed His love to the fullest, and, at the same time, realized it among us. Through Christ God challenged man to a covenant of friendship with Him; through Christ he finally established this covenant and leads it to its consummation. As the main messenger of His Father, Christ is "the Mediator and at the same time the fullness of all revelation" (CR, n.2; see also n.3).

Whenever the Council deals with a particular subject of great importance, it always presents it in the light of the saving plan of God which is the core of the Christian message. Classical examples of treating its great themes in their connection with the Mystery of Christ are, among others, the exposition of the mystery of the Church (CCH, nn. 1-8), the chapter on the nature of the sacred liturgy and its importance in the Church's life (CL, nn. 5-13), the passage upon "Christ as the New Man" in the Pastoral Constitution on the Church in the Modern World" (n. 22), the theological justification of the missionary activity of the Church (DM, nn. 2-5) and the introductory section of the Decree on Ecumenism (n. 2).

With great pastoral realism the Council realized that the lack of concentration in preconcilar catechists came above all from an inadequate training of the catechists, including the most qualified among them, the priests. Therefore in its Decree on Priestly Formation it insists that ecclesiastical studies from their very start "must work together harmoniously to unfold ever increasingly to the minds of the seminarians the mystery of Christ." "That this understanding may be communicated to students from the very start of their training, ecclesiastical studies should begin with an introductory course of suitable duration. In this initiation, the mystery of salvation should be presented in such a way that the students will see the meaning of ecclesiastical studies, their interrelationship, and their pastoral intent. They will be helped thereby to root their whole personal lives in faith and to permeate them with it. They will be strengthened to embrace their vocation with personal commitment and a joyful heart" (n. 14).

What the Council insists upon here must be applied to the formation of all the catechists. There must always be given special emphasis to the core of the Christian message. From the beginning of his formation, the catechist must learn to see and to evaluate all the rest in the light of this center. At the same time he must convince himself that this core of the message also lays down the basis for a truly Christian life. With St. Paul, the outstanding catechist of the apostolic Church, the Council calls this nucleus of the Christian message the MYSTERY OF CHRIST or the mystery of salvation. Like any technical expression, of course, the "Mystery of Christ" must be avoided in elementary catechesis.

2. Saint Paul, the herald of the Mystery of Christ

The teaching of St. Paul, as is well known, distinguishes itself by doctrinal richness. But it is precisely he who even more than the other apostles does not consider himself entrusted with a multitude of various doctrines, but with one fundamental message which includes all the rest; namely, what he calls time and time again "the" mystery or also the Mystery of Christ.

In proclaiming well this mystery, St. Paul sees the fulfillment of his whole apostolate (Col 4:3f). It is his special privilege "not only of proclaiming to the pagans the infinite treasure of Christ, but also of explaining how the mystery is to be dispensed . . . how comprehensive God's wisdom really is, exactly according to the plan which he had had from all eternity in Christ Jesus our Lord" (Eph 3:8-11; see the whole text 3:2-11). This mystery comprises all the rest, since in it "all the jewels and knowledge are hidden" (Col 2:3). Basically it is the mystery of God the Father (Col 2:2) who through Christ reveals and communicates Himself to us. It means the saving plan of God the Father which has been fulfilled through the coming and work of Christ.

With special enthusiasm, the Apostle speaks about this design of God in the first three chapters of his epistle to the Ephesians. Already at the very beginning of this letter, he lets us know what precisely he means by the Mystery of Christ. "Blessed be God the Father of Our Lord Jesus Christ, who has blessed us with all the spiritual blessings of heaven in Christ. Before the world was made, he chose us, chose us in Christ, to be holy and spotless, and to live through love in his presence, determining that we should become his adopted sons, through Jesus Christ for his own kind purposes, to make us praise the glory of his grace, his free gift to us in the Beloved, in whom, through his blood, we gain our freedom, the forgiveness of our sins. Such is the richness of the grace which he has showered on us in all wisdom and insight. He has let us know the mystery of his purpose, the hidden plan he so kindly made in Christ from the beginning to act upon when the times had run their course to the end: that he would bring everything together under Christ, as head, everything in the heavens and everything on earth" (Eph 1:3-10).

The realization of this loving design already began to prepare itself in the Old Covenant (cf. Rm 16:25f), and came to its fulfillment with the coming of Christ; it means a present reality for all those who accept the love of God and will reach its final consummation with the coming of Christ in glory (cf. Col 1:27). The whole is the invention of the Father's love and leads to the glory of God the Father (cf. Rm 16:27).

At the end of his career, St. Paul, explicitly characterizes the aim and content of his whole work in his farewell talk to the elders of Ephesus: "But life to me is not a thing to waste words on provided that when I finish my race I have carried out the mission the Lord Jesus gave me—and that was to bear witness to the Good News of God's grace . . . for I have without faltering put before you the whole of God's purpose" (Acts 20:24-27).

3. Characteristic features of the Christian message

With his continuous insistence on the central mystery, St. Paul only expresses with special emphasis what characterizes the whole message of the New Testament. With particular lucidity he renders prominent the features characteristic for any presentation of the Christian message which is truly Christian. What the Apostle calls "the" Mystery is not some speculative idea, but the invention of God's wisdom in order to manifest his infinite love by divine deeds. This plan, it is true, surpasses by far human expectation and speculation. Only God could devise and realize it. The whole Old Testament must be seen in the light of God's saving plan, although only as "guardian until Christ came" (Gal 3:24). "When the fullness of time had come" (Gal 4:4) God the heavenly Father finally revealed us fully and realized in our midst the design of His overwhelming love through Jesus Christ, setting us free from the slavery of sin, law and death through the passion and resurrection of His Son, and calling us to the freedom of His very children. That we can respond appropriately to His love, He sent together with His Son the Holy Spirit who lets us live as true children of God (Gal 4:4-6).

The realization of this divine design presents itself as the great *drama of love* between God and man in which we are not mere spectators but all important actors. In this way the central theme of the Christian message is the grandiose design of God which has its center in Christ and is intended for the good of man, in order to invite and accept him in a union of love (CR, n.2).

In order to understand and to present effectively God's plan of salvation, three different aspects of it must be distinguished clearly, three dimensions as it were, which thoroughly differ from one another, and, at the same time, complement one another. Many defects of inadequate catechesis result from not distinguishing clearly these three dimensions.

Under the aspect of the principle and end, the divine design is definitely *Fathercentered* (Godcentered). God the Father plans it and realizes it. The Father sends us His Son and calls and saves us through him. In order to lead us to His Father, the Son becomes man. At the end of his work of salvation the Son will "hand over the kingdom to God the Father . . . so that God may be all in all" (1 Co 15:24-28). Because the Christian message is basically the message of Father's love, it can only be answered by a thoroughly fathercentered spirituality which the Holy Spirit fosters within us: "Abba, Father!" (Gal 4:6; Rm 8:15).

Under the aspect of the main means through which God the Father has revealed and realized His love the Christian message is *Christcentered.* At the same time, Christ is also the most perfect expression of Father's love. Christ is the main gift of the Father and the unique mediator who leads us to the Father. "Yes, God loved the world so much that he gave his only Son, so that everyone who believes in him may not be lost but may have eternal life" (Jn 3:16). "For there is only one God, and there is only one mediator between God and mankind, himself a man, Jesus Christ, who sacrificed himself for them all" (1 Tm 2:5f). Therefore, "eternal life is this: to know you, the only true God, and Jesus Christ whom you have sent" (Jn 17:3), the Father as the principle and end, and the Son as the only way to the Father. It is exactly this that Christ inculcates in his testament: "I am the Way, the Truth and the Life. No one can come to the Father except through me" (Jn 14:6).

Any kind of catechesis or piety which stops in fact with Christ and does not follow him to the Father contradicts obviously both the emphasis of the Bible and the fundamental orientation of the whole liturgy. In its official cult the Church shows us authentically how we have to answer to God's call. Since the times of the Apostles the prayer of the Church as a whole ascends through Christ to the Father in the Holy Spirit who unites us with Christ and imbues us with his filial attitude.

Under the aspect of the recipient and beneficiary, the Christian message is intended for man. In this sense it can be called *mancentered.* The whole divine revelation and the whole work of salvation addresses itself to man, it is planned "for us men and for our salvation" (Credo). It is by no means an impersonal "perennial" message broadcasted into a celestial vacuum, but a message of love which aims at concrete man in his historic existence and situation and challenges him to a union of love with God forever. More than any other Council, Vatican II has in its whole work insisted upon this human dimension, most especially in its longest and most significant document, the Pastoral Constitution on the Church in the Modern World. The same emphasis we find in the GCD: "Catechesis must, then, show clearly the very close connection of the mystery of God and Christ with man's existence and his ultimate end. This in no way implies any contempt for the earthly goals which men are divinely called to pursue by individual or common efforts; it does, however, clearly teach that man's ultimate end is not confined to these temporal goals, but rather surpasses them beyond all expectation, to a degree that only God's love for men could make possible" (n. 42, see also the preceding nn. 39-41 in which the GCD stresses the theocentricity and christocentricity of the Christian message together with the necessity of presenting it as an organic whole with true emphasis upon the core of the whole Christian message).

AIDS FOR DISCUSSION AND ASSIMILATION

1. *What do we mean by lack of catechetical concentration?*
2. *How did the Council try to remedy the former lack of catechetical concentration?*
3. *What do we mean by the MYSTERY OF CHRIST?*
4. *In what sense is the Christian message GOD-centered, CHRIST-centered, MAN-centered?*

> A catechesis that neglects this interrelation and harmony of its content can become entirely useless for achieving its proper end (General Catechetical Directory, n. 39).

3

Searching for God

Has God intended His message of love for everyone? Are all disposed to receive this message? What can we do to help prepare people for God's word?

In His loving concern for man, God "wants everyone to be saved and reach full knowledge of truth" (I Tm 2:5). After having spoken in the past through the prophets, He finally spoke to us "through His Son, the Son He has appointed to inherit everything" (Heb 1:2). God's eagerness to communicate with man is very often not met by man's corresponding eagerness to listen to God and to communicate with Him.

There have always been plenty of individuals who cared very little for God's saving word. Without explicitly denying it, they would just neglect God in planning and arranging their lives. Yet, in our times, we find an even more general disinterest in religion and a strong trend towards resolute atheism and the occult. This makes it even more difficult to present Christian message to man of today.

1. Admit the presence of religious indifferentism and atheism

Whatever the religious situation may have been in the past, at least in our times, catechesis "cannot ignore the fact that not a few men of our era strongly sense a remoteness and even absence of God" (GCD, n. 48). "Many of our contemporaries recognize in no way this intimate and vital link with God, or else they explicitly reject it. Thus atheism must be accounted among the most serious problems of this age, and must be subjected to closer examination" (CMW, n. 19; GCD, 7). "That form of civilization which is called scientific, technical, industrial, and urban not infrequently diverts the attention of men from matters divine and makes their inner concerns with regard to religion more difficult. Many feel that God is less present, and less needed, and God seems to them less able to explain things in both personal and social life. . . . This situation calls for pastoral remedies that are truly adapted to the circumstances" (GCD, n. 5). The new situation cannot be met by mere intensification of catechetical efforts in the traditional style, rather it demands that "the catechetical plan be thoroughly renewed" (GCD, n. 9).

In this situation of today we cannot just concentrate on the ever shrinking group of faithful who, until now, are not yet deeply influenced by the process of secularization and appear rather unimpressed by the ideals and aspirations of the modern mind, writing off all the other as unworthy and incapable of accepting the gospel of Christ. But we can also not treat these others as faithful, wrongly supposing that the mere fact of baptism guarantees in some way the basic disposition of faith. We must first help them to accept God in their lives and to commit themselves to Him in a faith which gives a new meaning to their lives. Without preparing adequately the ground for God's message, any presentation of the mysteries of God's love would achieve very little positive results; on the contrary, in most of the cases it would do more harm than good. This is of paramount importance in the catechesis of teenagers, especially, if they have been pressured to participate in a religious education program.

In such cases it is wrong and harmful to insist that the youngsters should be given a detailed exposition of the Christian message without allowing the catechist to lay first the necessary foundation. In our times the basic experience and attitude of faith can no longer be generally presupposed in youth who come from traditionally Catholic families, nor even in those who regularly participate in the life of the Church.

The remoteness and absence of God in modern society, "which is a part of the process of secularization, surely constitutes a danger for the faith; but it also impells us to have a purer faith and to become more humble in the presence of the mystery of God, as we ought" (GCD, n. 48). It forces us to stress even more than in the past our basic relationship to God by entrusting our very self to God (cf. CR, n. 5) and to consider faith as a precious gift of God for which we owe Him deep gratitude and which we have to preserve and ever more to develop diligently (see GCD, n. 3).

2. Help to find God in life

In helping our brethren who have lost all vital contact with God or who have even deliberately banished Him from their basic decisions, we should learn from the Council. "While rejecting atheism, root and branch," the Church "still strives to detect in the atheistic mind the hidden causes for the denial of God. Conscious of how weighty are the questions which atheism raises, and motivated by love for all men, she believes these questions ought to be examined seriously and more profoundly" (CMW, n. 21). Any meaningful help which we give people who live without God, supposes the endeavor to understand them. That "cannot be realized apart from sincere and prudent dialogue" (CMW, n. 21).

Quite often the difficulties in accepting God in their lives result from unsatisfactory teaching about God and His place in human life. What is resolutely rejected is not so much God Himself as the poor image of God presented to them by incompetent messengers of God. And what irritates them even more is usually the contradiction they find, or believe to find, between what Christians say about God and what they do in their lives.

Therefore, we have quite often to *clear the way* to God first by removing the main obstacles and misunderstandings. Among the misunderstandings which bar the acceptance of God by modern man, the Council mentions three of special importance. With the Council we must help modern man to understand that a godcentered outlook of life is not an abdication of his own freedom, but the very foundation and indispensable safeguard for true creative freedom and the most effective protection against freedom's degeneration into egoistic and vile arbitrariness (see CMW, n. 20).

Likewise, "the recognition of God is in no way hostile to man's dignity, since this dignity is rooted and perfected in God. For man was made an intelligent and free member of society by the God who created him. Even more importantly, man is called as a son to commune with God and to share in His happiness" (CMW, n. 21).

Finally, modern man seeks his full human development and liberation from unhealthly economic and social entanglements. He fears, however, "that by its very nature religion thwarts such liberation by arousing man's hope for a deceptive future life, thereby diverting him from the constructing of the earthly city" (CMW, n. 20). In response to this view, the Council stresses the seriousness of our temporal commitment. At the same time it rightly insists that "a hope related to the end of time does not diminish the importance of intervening duties, but rather undergirds the acquittal of them with fresh incentives" (CMW, n. 21).

When speaking to modern man about God we must *present him with an image of God he can truly appreciate.* It must fit in without unnecessary friction into the concept of the world he has received from modern science, but must further deepen it and lead it to its final unity.

Modern man refuses any kind of religion which offers itself as a substitute for his task to control and master the powers of nature by his own studies and efforts. He definitely would prefer to live at the mercy of blind powers which, until now, he has not yet brought sufficiently under his control rather than take refuge in a God who is retreating from this world in the very measure science progresses.

The only type of God that is acceptable to modern man is a God who under every aspect transcends this visible world, including man himself, and at the same time is the very root and deepest reason for everything we encounter in human life.

We do not expect that modern man will blindly accept God in his life. We *must present reasons.* But we never must give the impression that we can prove the existence of God in the way as we prove facts in history and natural science or as we arrive at mathematical conclusions. It is the interpretation of world and life which leads to God as the only satisfactory explanation. People who do not care about the meaning of the world and life will not find Him at all.

Mere theoretical reasons do not impress the man of today. He almost never finds and accepts God in his own life without the convincing experience of a living and mature faith which he encounters in his life (see CMW, n. 21; GCD, n. 7).

In our times we find everywhere a good number of people who consider the occult as a rewarding *substitute for religion.* They turn to all kinds of spiritism, witchcraft and satanism. Countless others hope to find God and meaning for their lives outside of any institutionalized form of religion. They may enthusiastically accept Christ, but resolutely reject belonging to any Church. We cannot overlook them, but we also cannot treat them like atheists. We usually find them very little disposed to listen to reasons. They are looking for a way of life which satisfies the deep emotional aspirations of man without imposing any binding religious commitment. Considering their mentality, we can hardly help them find the right way to God except by opening the way to deep and genuine religious experience within a community of faith and love with a maximum of communion and a minimum of institutionalization.

There they should find the necessary deepening and maturation for their religious aspirations.

Modern man *does not want to be pushed.* We must give him time. We may give him helpful hints for finding his way, yet, he must finally do it himself. We may suggest themes for reflection and at most insinuate meaningful conclusions. Every human situation and problem of any depth has its open end pointing to God as the deepest root and final fulfillment of our life.

With great brotherly love we must try to understand, we must even consider it our privilege to serve as we pray, but we must never judge. From the Council we know that sincere searchers are already on the way of salvation. "Those also can attain to everlasting salvation who through no fault of their own do not know the gospel of Christ or his Church, yet sincerely seek God and, moved by grace, strive by their own deeds to do His will as it is known to them through the dictates of conscience" (CCH, n. 16). Better a man who in this way searches for God than a Catholic who by his own fault does not appreciate the gift of faith. Nevertheless, it is only in a real community of faith that truly mature faith is able to develop. Substitutes are sought only when one is not able to find such a community of committed Christians.

AIDS FOR DISCUSSION AND ASSIMILATION

1. *Why is it more difficult for man of today to accept God in his life?*
2. *Why must we first prepare the ground before presenting the mysteries of God's love?*
3. *How can we help unbelievers on their way to God?*
4. *What idea of God appeals to modern man?*

> The greatest way the faithful can help the atheistic world for coming to God is by the witness of a life which agrees with the message of Christ's love and of a living and mature faith that is manifested by works of justice and charity (General Catechetical Directory, n. 49).

4

How to Arrange the Catechetical Material

How should the particular doctrines be arranged in order to communicate clearly God's message of love? Is there any arrangement which deserves prior consideration in a first initiation of adults?

Whatever the catechist teaches, he must present his particular topic in such a way that the main idea of God's revelation, His eternal love for men manifested and realized in Jesus Christ, clearly shines forth and leads ever more efficiently to a grateful response of love. And this grateful response must show in man's whole life. In each catechetical instruction, therefore, the connection between the particular topic and God's saving love must be apparent.

In order to be properly understood and evaluated, parts of a whole must be viewed in their function within and their connection with the whole; think, for example, about the parts of a whole construction like doors, windows or the roof. The same holds also for understanding and evaluating properly any particular doctrine of the whole Christian message.

Whenever not only one particular doctrine, but a substantial part of the Christian message, or even a summary of the whole Christian message is to be presented, the problem arises as to how to arrange the catechetical material in order to show as strikingly as possible its inner unity as the message of God's love.

Particular doctrines can be arranged in various ways. When the GCD deals with the basic norms for presenting the catechetical content it concludes with the following comment: "It is not possible, however, to deduce from these norms an order which must be followed in the exposition of the content. It is right to begin with God and proceed to Christ, or to do the reverse;

similarly, it is permissible to begin with man and proceed to God, or to do the reverse, and so on. In selecting a pedagogical method, one ought to take into account the circumstances in which the ecclesial community or the individuals among the faithful to whom the catechesis is directed live. From this there arises the need to use great diligence in looking into and finding ways and methods which better respond to the various circumstances" (GCD, n. 46).

According to the particular situation of those to be catechized special aspects of the Christian religion may need to be emphasized and the grouping of the particular doctrines determined. Sometimes we may bring to the foreground the community aspect of the Christian message, on another occasion it may be appropriate to show God's saving plan under the aspect of man's call to perfect freedom in Christ. But ultimately it is always God's loving concern for man that has to shine forth and the way by which God achieves His plan through Jesus Christ.

For an initiation of adults into a deeper understanding of God's plan for mankind, the best, the most simple and natural arrangement is one which follows closely the inner dynamics of God's revelation. This is the *genetic approach.* It shows how God's friendship with man started, progressed and is to be consummated at the end of time, presenting in fact the dramatic story of God's love for man. This arrangement is recommended, since it flows from God's own presentation in his "catechism," the Bible. It is most adapted to the intelligence of people without special professional training. It is closest to our experience in life, where we find friendship as one of life's most exciting and challenging experiences.

In using this approach, one must show the dramatic character (tensions and oppositions) of this story of love. One must show its dialogical nature (call and answer, active involvement of both partners, God and man). And one must show its actuality (its relevance for our life here and now). What interests us is not the history of the past, but our own experience of God, is love which enlightens our life here and now, and opens us to an even greater future.

The main parts, or acts in the great "drama" of God's love are:

1. *The dramatic start* of God's friendship with man: Creation and first call–God's first "yes" to man, man's "no" to God's

love (sin)—God's saving mercy (sin overpowered by God's love), promising the Savior to come.

2. *Salvation prepared*—Old Testament.
3. *Salvation offered*—The coming of Christ; his saving acts during his earthly life, crowned by his resurrection.
4. *Salvation achieved*—By Christ, here and now, with us, in the Church.
5. *Salvation consummated*—Second coming of Christ, fulfillment in Christ.

AIDS FOR DISCUSSION AND ASSIMILATION

1. *What are the basic requirements for any good arrangement of the catechetical material?*
2. *What do you mean by the "genetic approach" in arranging the catechetical material?*
3. *Can you give any reasons which recommend the genetic approach?*
4. *What do you mean by showing the "dramatic character," the "dialogical nature" and the "actuality" of God's friendship with man?*
5. *What are the main parts in the "drama" of God's love with man?*

> The object of faith embraces a content which of its very nature is complex, namely, God in his own mystery and in his saving intervention in history. All these things are known through what God himself has revealed about himself and about his works. Christ has central importance both in the salvific intervention of God and in the manifestation of him to men. Catechesis, therefore, has as object God's mystery and works, namely, the works that God has done, is doing, and will do for us men and for our salvation (General Catechetical Directory, n. 39).

5
How to Teach About God

How does God in His own book speak about Himself? What must be stressed more particularly when speaking about God?

1. The starting point

Catechisms of old usually started with a long and rather abstract chapter about God, the one and triune. In the Bible the starting point is God's work for us—how he made the world for mankind and man; from the visible work of God, we are to understand and to appreciate God himself, whom we cannot see. But, the point to be reached is always God and our way to God, and not just a "godly" thing or person.

A fundamental law of genuine catechesis is this: Start with the visible—what we can grasp with our senses—the concrete, a story or a picture or an experience in daily life. But in each particular catechesis lead up to God himself, and our way to God. Never make your stopping point, or your final aim, godly things, like sacramentals, or godly persons, saints. Good catechesis must be GODCENTERED. The main reason catechesis so often is not sufficiently Godcentered is that the spiritual life of the catechist is not really Godcentered.

2. The importance of conveying a truly magnificent idea of God

It is imperative to lead to a religious attitude that permeates all aspects of life. For religion essentially consists in acknowledging the absolute excellence of God and our complete dependence on him. An idea of the greatness of God is *the first of the two main pillars* of our Christian religion: the Great God—our Father in Christ. A lack of this foundation necessarily results in a lack of vigor in our entire religious life. No one wants to try to do great things for an insignificant God. We simply cannot appreciate the basic teachings of Christianity if we lack an awareness of the greatness of God: the person and work of Christ, the God-man, grace as God's life in us, sin as our "no" to God, heaven as our final union with God, etc.

3. What is to be especially emphasized when speaking of God

a) *Reality and nearness of God.* He is not an abstract idea, just a postulate of philosophy that leaves us cold, but he is the Reality of realities with which we have to deal in our life, which reveals him everywhere and at any moment, the One who gives meaning to our life. "In Him we live and move and have our being" (Acts 17:28). Reality means more than mere existence, it stresses his relevance for us. Only with a God who is relevant and near to us we can dialogue in personal prayer.

Should we "prove" God's existence? Not in a dry apologetical approach. We should instead offer—according to the needs of the audience—convincing reasons why we accept God in our life as the great Reality, and lead to a personal experience of His presence by creating an atmosphere where prayer is possible.

b) *The greatness and transcendence of God.* We should try to communicate how much greater and better God is than anything we find here on earth, that he is without limits, that he surpasses essentially all his work. God's greatness must be studied in all subjects, arts and sciences. The whole of creation speaks of its Master. Finally, *God is greatest in his love.* His absolutely selfless love surpasses any love a human being can have for another. "Even if a mother should forget her child . . . I will never forget you!" (Is 49:15). Awareness of God's transcendence motivates our attitude of deepest admiration and reverence; God's love wins our hearts and prevents our awe from degenerating into fear and reserve.

c) *Our absolute dependence on God.* We depend upon Him much more completely than a sunbeam on the sun, than a newborn baby on his mother. The worst thing we could ever attempt to do would be to try to escape Him. This would be impossible and foolish at the same time, since no one loves us as much and as sincerely as God does. God is the only one who can never abuse His authority. No one is so concerned about helping us grow according to our individuality as God who made us in this very way. His authority is always in the service of His love. In order to understand and appreciate God's friendship with man properly, it must be pondered in the light of His transcendence and authority.

AIDS FOR DISCUSSION AND ASSIMILATION

1. *What does Godcentered catechesis mean?*
2. *Why is it so important to convey a truly magnificent idea of God?*
3. *Why have we in teaching about God to stress in a special way His reality, nearness, transcendence, love and authority?*

"Yes, naturally stupid are all men who have not known God and who, from the good things that are seen, have not been able to discover Him-who-is, or, by studying the works, have failed to recognize the Artificer" (Ws 13:1; see also Rm 1:19-20). In searching for God "the right use of human reason may not be neglected; for, as the Church holds and teaches, from created things this reason can come to a knowledge of God as the beginning and the end of all things (cf. First Vatican Council, Dogm. Const. *Dei Filius,* Dz.-Sch., 3004-3005, 3026). This knowledge of God not only does no harm to human dignity, but rather gives it a basis and strength" (General Catechetical Directory, n. 49).

6

Creation: The First Act in the Drama of God's Love for Man

Is true religion only concerned with God, or also with man and human life? What does God tell us in the first chapter of His book about man and God's concern for man? How is man to meet the challenge of God's creative love?

In every true deep friendship, beginnings are very significant. They mean much to both friends and will be remembered throughout the experience of friendship. This is true in the case of God's friendship with man. God's first "yes" to man was *creation.* So, creation must be presented as the first splendid manifestation of God's love.

1. Creation: The work of God's abundant and self-giving love

a) *Man: God's Masterpiece.* The whole of creation is good, made for man placed as master over the visible creation. Man—made in God's image—is "very" god (Gen 1:31). Man's similarity to God, based on his nature as intelligent and free being reaches its final consummation in Jesus Christ, the God-man and in our union with Christ in the Holy Spirit.

b) *Transcendence of Man.* Man's excellence consists in his special similarity to God. Only man can reflect; can make a free choice; can freely realize himself. Only man is capable of true dialogue and of free collaboration with God. Only man can understand God's plan, can evaluate, can accept, can refuse this plan. The total greatness of man consists in his capacity for dialogue and free friendship with God. The tragic consequence of his freedom is his ability to refuse God's love, his ability to say "no" to God, and in doing this, saying "no" to himself. Gen 1:26-28.

Any conception of life which does not firmly establish man's freedom, degrades man to a mere object of his environment and deprives him of his dignity as a person (cf. GCD, 61). But freedom is not to be considered as a gift which God gave to man from the very beginning in its final perfection. According to God's plan, man must make himself ever more free, with God's help he has to liberate himself. Here we touch the very root of any sound and relevant "catechesis of liberation." It would be a mistake to think that the worst obstacles to man's freedom come from without. But it would be equally wrong to minimize the disastrous consequences which exterior oppression and misery have upon the exercise and development of true human freedom.

Only man can understand and accept himself as the gift of God's creative love. The meaning of his life, therefore, can only be to give himself to God by a life of thankful love.

c) *The First Dialogue of Love* (Gen 1:29-31). As soon as God has made man, he begins his dialogue: "Behold, I have given you. . . ." In his love, God, from the very beginning, wants to share with man, wants to make him happy, plans true prosperity for man already here on earth. But, this earthly prosperity must be accepted and appreciated as the gift of God's love. As truly human prosperity, it presupposes man's free collaboration with God's plan. This means well planned and well organized work: God's "yes" to modern technology and science–man's strict obligation to work for the betterment of the world! It means just distribution of the goods which result from human work and brotherly collaboration, not just thinking of personal enrichment and neglecting the community. The earthly prosperity which necessarily results from fulfilling these conditions must be understood as an anticipation (appetizer) of man's final and consummate happiness which will be given to him as the gift of God's love. It will be given, of course, provided he says "yes" to God's plan in his life.

2. Some important qualities of any good catechesis illustrated by the doctrine of creation

It must be:

a) *Concrete:* Starting from the visible and from the experiences of human life.

b) *Realistic:* Integrating well what the students learn in science, for example, on evolution and what they learn in sociology on equal dignity and rights of man and woman and of the various races.

c) *Optimistic:* Showing how the world and man are *basically* good. Man is made for prosperity and it begins here on earth. But this optimism must be realistic, stressing the need for man's work in mutual collaboration, and aware of the possibility of his saying "no" to God's love.

d) *Personal:* Presenting religion as a free dialogue with God, both as individual person and as a community (ecclesial dimension).

e) *Integral:* Showing how this particular doctrine fits into the whole drama of God's love. For example, pointing out that creation is the "first act," followed by man's tragic "no," which on its part occasioned God's greatest manifestation of His "superabundant" (Rm 5:20) love by sending us His Son as Savior (Cf. GCD, n. 51 #3).

Integral catechesis also calls for the harmonious integration of material and temporal values and of the community aspect into the presentation of God's saving plan. God's plan concerns the whole of mankind, represented by our first parents (consider their names!). Nobody saves himself in a spiritual desert, but only by his integration into the saving community.

AIDS FOR DISCUSSION AND ASSIMILATION

1. In what consists man's greatness and in what his tragedy?
2. How does creation prove God's love?

3. *What are some of the main conditions for man's well-being here on earth?*
4. *In what sense is it man's task to liberate himself? What is meant by a catechesis of "liberation"?*
5. *Enumerate and explain some of the more important qualities of good catechesis and illustrate them with the doctrine on creation.*

The truth of creation is not to be presented simply as a truth standing by itself, torn from the rest, but as something which is in fact ordered to the salvation wrought by Jesus Christ. The creation of visible and invisible things, of the world and of angels, is the beginning of the mystery of salvation (cf. DV, 3); the creation of man (cf. Pius XII, Encycl. *Humani generis, AAS,* 1950, p. 575; GS, 12, 14) is to be regarded as the first gift and the first call that leads to glorification in Christ (cf. Rom. 8, 29-30). When a Christian hears the explanation of the doctrine about creation, besides thinking about the first act whereby God "created the heavens and the earth" (Gen. 1, 1), he should turn his mind to all the salvific undertakings of God. These things are always present in the history of man and of the world; they also shine forth especially in the history of Israel; they lead to the supreme event of Christ's resurrection; and, finally, they will be brought to completion at the end of the world, when there will be "new heavens and a new earth" (cf. 2 Pet. 3, 13) (General Catechetical Directory, n. 51).

7

Man's "No" to God's Love: Sin

Would it perhaps not be better to leave out completely the topic of sin from catechesis which is, after all, Good News? What has the teaching on sin to do with the message of God's love?

Man unfortunately did not accept God's love as he should have done. From the beginning and throughout the centuries man has refused God's love and has sinned. Catechesis of old quite often spoke too much and, usually, too early of sin. In our times we come across the other, equally wrong extreme of speaking too little of sin or of speaking too late of it.

1) *Sin is a sad, but undeniable fact* which we cannot conceal. We simply cannot present a true, realistic picture of man and his life with God without speaking clearly on sin. Further, we cannot show the unfathomable love of God. The central idea of Christian religion, of Christian faith is precisely the victory of God's love over man's selfishness and malice which we encounter all along the history of mankind (see Col 1:33 ff). "The profound reflections found in St. Paul (cf. Rm 5) concerning the reality of sin and Christ's consequent 'work of justice' must be numbered among the principal points of the Christian faith, and it is not right to pass over them in silence in catechesis" (GCD, n. 62, #3). Cf. also 1 Jn 1:8-2:2.

2) *The emphasis must be on personal sin,* with its individual and social aspects, and not on original sin. It is much easier to understand personal sin—the only kind of sin we find in our own life experience; further, the knowledge and recognition and the renunciation of personal sin is also much more important. Only personal sin clarifies the meaning of sin: a deliberate rejection of God's love (mortal sin), or resistance against God's love (venial sin).

3) *We can speak of sin even to children of 6 or 7 years,* but without stressing the word. We should not mention at that age the story of sin in the Garden of Paradise, much less should we mention mortal sin and hell. The first presentation must be very personal, on the level of their experience, not legalistic, not as transgression of the law but as a saying "no" to God. We can use the comparison of children having a wrong attitude towards their own parents in their family.

4) *Children do not commit mortal sins.* They can commit, now and then, very bad exterior acts, but they cannot fully understand nor evaluate their moral malice. They have not yet sufficiently developed moral responsibility to commit themselves and to break a real commitment.

5) *Presenting mortal sin* for the first time: Perhaps we could begin to teach these doctrines at the age of ten, but even at this age, we must take care that the children do not think that their usual sins are mortal. For example, in this first presentation, we must never use sins against the 3rd and 6th commandments. Rather, we should use examples of sins children can sufficiently understand and evaluate, but not easily commit, like a "big" robbery, murder, drug pushing. Show as clearly as possible how sin is never committed by hand or foot, but only by the heart (will); that is, deliberately and freely revolting against God.

6) *How to distinguish mortal sin from venial sin.* The paramount difference between venial sin and mortal sin can be explained best in terms of friendship. In any true friendship every deliberate offense of the friend is really bad but not every offense breaks the bounds of friendship. There are no venial sins in the sense of insignificant, negligible sins. In the light of God's love every deliberate sin is very bad. What would you think, for example, of a housewife who knowing the taste of her husband deliberately puts too much salt in the soup against his liking? Would such an attitude and action not badly hinder their life of love? Nevertheless it would not, in itself, sever their married friendship. Only mortal sin breaks our friendship with God. It is a fully deliberated rejection of His love, a fundamental option against God in our life.

Whenever we speak of sin, we have always to stress how it displeases God and how God manifests His dissatisfaction by punishing sin. But whenever He punishes, again He wants to help us like a loving father. Every sin consists in shameful selfishness. Even when there is no punishment from without, selfish people make themselves unhappy, unwanted and bad.

7) *Sin has a role of transition in catechesis.* It is never the point at which we start, much less the point at which we end. We begin with God's love and end with God's love. God used man's ingratitude to manifest His love, even more superabundantly (Rm 5:20). But when we speak of sin, we must always stress how sin displeases God. God hates sin, but loves the sinner and calls him to repentance. Parables of the Good Shepherd (Lk 15:1-7) and the Prodigal Son (Lc 15:11-32).

AIDS FOR DISCUSSION AND ASSIMILATION

1. *Why do we speak of sin in our catechesis?*
2. *At what age may we mention sin to the children for the first time? What is the best approach to use?*
3. *Do children commit mortal sins? Why not?*
4. *How do we distinguish mortal and venial sins?*
5. *At what age may we start speaking to the children of mortal sin? What is the best approach to use?*
6. *What is the place of sin in good catechesis?*

> If we say that we have no sin, we deceive ourselves and there is no truth in us. But if we confess our sins to God, we can trust him, for he does what is right—he will forgive us our sins and make us clean from all our wrongdoing. If we say that we have not sinned, we make a liar out of God, and his word is not in us. I write you this, my children, so that you will not sin; but if anyone does sin, we have Jesus Christ, the righteous, who pleads for us with the Father. For Christ himself is the means by which our sins are forgiven, and not our sins only, but also the sins of all men (1 Jn 1:8–2:2).

8

Man's Final and Definite "No" to God: Hell

What happens to man if he finally and definitely refuses God's love? Should we still speak of hell in catechesis? How to integrate the doctrine on hell harmoniously into the gospel of God's saving love?

Man is free to accept or to refuse God's love. If he finally and definitively refuses God's love, he will end up in a state of self-chosen loneliness and rejection, and that is what we call hell.

We do not speak of hell to little children, but when we speak of mortal sin, we must also speak of hell. As faithful messengers of Christ, we are not allowed to suppress doctrines he has taught very clearly. But we must also carefully avoid any wrong emphasis on the doctrine of hell. And when we speak of this doctrine, like any other doctrine, it must be *well integrated into the whole message of God's saving love.*

1. Why did Jesus speak of hell?

To bring out God's love and mercy and the reality of the gift of freedom. God revealed hell in order to call sinners to repentance. So whenever we speak of hell, we too must act as instruments of God's love and mercy, calling the sinner to true repentance. By speaking of hell, we are supposed not to "open" hell, but close it! Every instruction on hell should be an impressive presentation of God's mercy, being offered to the sinner.

2. What did Christ say about hell?

What does the doctrine of hell mean? The imagery of the Bible can only be used and explained well if we understand its real meaning. It wants to say: Whoever rejects God's love in selfishness and permanently decides against God will end up in a state of separation from God forever. This destroys all his happiness and inflicts unspeakable pain. Christ clearly distinguishes a twofold aspect: separation and torments. "Then he will say to those on his left: Away from me, you that are under God's curse! Away to the eternal fire which has been prepared for the devil and his angels" (Mt 25:41). "Then the king told the servants: Tie him up hand and foot and throw him outside in the dark. There he will cry and gnash his teeth" (Mt 22:13). Of these two aspects, that of separation is surely the most tragic. Why does the emphasis on fire appear in Scripture? The answer to that is that God wants to win back the selfish sinner. In his selfishness, man does not appreciate God. Separation from God does not impress him. So God uses language adapted to man and to his selfishness and speaks of pains and torments. *What of this fire?* Of course, it is not fire like we have in our stoves! It means that all creatures will necessarily turn into instruments (causes) of torment for him who has definitively rejected God who is the cause of all joy and happiness. Compare this with the situation of a man looking at the photograph of a formerly loved person after their friendship has been broken and has become mutual hatred. The fire of hell is the only fire which cannot be called "brother" fire in the meaning of St. Francis of Assisi.

3. Who goes to hell?

Never speak of hell without making it clear who goes to hell. Only the one who has committed mortal sin (fully, deliberately, freely committed revolt against God) and now refuses to repent. There is nothing to be feared if only the sinner accepts God and God's mercy.

4. What has God personally done in order that we may avoid hell?

Present an adaptation of the parable of the Prodigal Son (Lk 15:11ff.). The heavenly fulfillment is much greater than the earthly reality. The Father does not only wait patiently; he secretly follows the sinner and gently draws him back (grace of repentance). In Jesus we find a most wonderful older brother. The Father sends him to bring the brother back. He finds him in misery. He convinces him of the Father's love. He takes upon himself the punishment which his prodigal brother deserved.

AIDS FOR DISCUSSION AND ASSIMILATION

1. *What does hell mean?*
2. *Why does God, and we in His name, speak of hell?*
3. *What are the main aspects of punishment in hell?*
4. *How do you understand the fire of hell?*
5. *Who goes to hell? Mention two conditions, and not only one.*
6. *What has God done, in order that we may avoid hell?*

All this is done by God, who through Christ changed us from enemies into his friends, and gave us the task of making others his friends also. Our message is that God was making friends of all men through Christ. God did not keep an account of their sins against them, and he has given us the message of how he makes them his friends.

Here we are, then, speaking for Christ, as though God himself were appealing to you through us: on Christ's behalf, we beg you, let God change you from enemies into friends! Christ was without sin, but for our sake God made him share our sin in order that we, in union with him, might share the righteousness of God (2 Co 5:18-21).

9

Man's Revolt Against God Since the Beginning: Original Sin

What do you think of catechists who do not speak of original sin anymore? How can we make the doctrine of original sin meaningful to modern man?

It is not only occasionally that man rejects God's love. From the beginning of mankind, we find sin pervading the whole history of man. Sin is not just a sporadic event in the life of man; rather, all of mankind is in a sinful condition, and that, from its very origins. This forces us to speak of original sin. The way that God, in fact, planned and achieved our salvation through Christ can only be understood in the fact of this universality of sin.

Some basic principles with regard to the teaching on original sin

1) The doctrine of original sin is *a part of God's revelation* which must be kept intact and presented to the faithful. "It is human nature fallen, stripped of grace that clothed it, injured in its own natural powers and subjected to the dominion of death, that is transmitted to all men, and it is in this sense that every man is born in sin" (Paul VI, Professio fidei, n. 16; see GCD, n. 62). It is not enough just to keep the name and substitute a completely different meaning. But, it is necessary to explain it in such a way that it does not contradict modern science, or the solid biblical studies of our times.

2) *In the classical explanation,* original sin was understood as the deliberate rejection of God's plan and love by the first

individual in human history, an individual named Adam. Because of the sin of this one single man all his descendants lost God's love and life. Original sin in us meant lack of God's life in man before his saving union with Christ in baptism. All of this, of course, resulting from the one actual sin of the one first sinner, Adam. The difficulty with this explanation is twofold: How could the first man in history–according to science, obviously an extremely primitive man–be responsible for all following men? And, does not the very name, "Adam" imply that we are to understand him as representing all mankind, that is, everyone?

3) *Perhaps the following explanation would avoid these difficulties* and at the same time, preserve the substance of Catholic doctrine. This must be understood as a theological explanation of the dogma, not as the Church's established doctrine. According to it Adam is a corporate person, the "Everyone," together with Eve, standing for the whole human race. The sin of Adam is not only that of one individual, but the sin (countless sins) of the whole lineage. From the outset God intended to share with man His very life. But because of man's continuous rebellion since the beginnings of his existence, God finds man positively unworthy of His friendship. Looking to this situation, one sees it as a situation of sin, devoid of God's life and special love. Because of our belonging to sinful mankind we enter the world deprived of God's life as originally meant to be given to us according to God's loving intention. Then, in order to manifest his "superabundant" (Rm 5:20) love and mercy, God sends His son, Jesus Christ. Now, whoever becomes united to Christ (faith–baptism) will receive God's love through Christ who is Savior. In this explanation, the doctrine of original sin is the useful (though negative) formulation of the basic Christian doctrine of the universality of Christ's grace: In this world, no one receives God's life except through Christ who has overcome our sin.

4) *The doctrine of original sin is a rather difficult doctrine.* It should not be presented explicitly to children who cannot sufficiently understand its real meaning. Rather than risk misunderstanding, it would be better to present it implicitly as it was, in fact, presented to all Christians in the first great centuries of the Church: God loved man from the very

beginning. But man did not accept God's love and revolted against God again and again. God, nevertheless, did not abandon man but sent His own Son as man's Savior. All who accept Christ will be made children of God through him.

AIDS FOR DISCUSSION AND ASSIMILATION

1. *What do you mean by Original Sin?*
2. *What is the main difference between the former and a solid new explanation?*
3. *How are we to present Original Sin "implicitly" to children?*

The history of salvation is also the history of liberation from sin. Every intervention of God both in the Old and in the New Testament was to give guidance to men in the struggle against the forces of sin. The role entrusted to Christ in the history of salvation relates to the destruction of sin, and is fulfilled through the mystery of the cross. The profound reflections found in St. Paul (cf. Rom. 5) concerning the reality of sin and Christ's consequent "work of justice" must be numbered among the principal points of the Christian faith, and it is not right to pass over them in silence in catechesis.

But the salvation brought by Jesus Christ involves much more than redemption from sin. For it fulfills the plan begun by God that he would communicate himself in Jesus with such fullness that it utterly transcends human understanding. The plan in question does not come to an end because of men's transgressions, but it confers a grace that is superabundant compared to the death which sin brought (cf. Rom. 5, 15-17). This plan, which has proceeded from love, by virtue of which men are called by the Holy Spirit to share in divine life itself, is always in force and belongs to all times. Even though man is a sinner, he always remains in the one order which God willed, namely, in the order in which God mercifully shares himself with us in Jesus Christ, and man can, therefore, under the impulse of grace, attain salvation through repentance (General Catechetical Directory, n. 62).

10

Preparing for the Coming Messiah: Old Testament

Has the Old Testament, being essentially a time of preparation for Christ, still relevance to us who live in the fullness of time? How are we to use the Old Testament in catechesis and Christian life?

In spite of the reality of sin throughout the thousands of years since man came into existence, God has continued to communicate his deep love for mankind. He prepared for man a unique opportunity for friendship with Himself. He would send them His very son as Savior. From the beginning, He inspired man to hope for a better future. The more time progressed, the clearer became the promise of the Savior. The first promise as we find it in Gn 3:15 is very vague. We can only understand it the light of the coming events, the coming Savior promised as the son of a great woman; this is the *Protoevangelium,* the first announcement of the coming Savior.

1. The Old Testament: A time of preparation

In the first years of elementary grades we speak little of the Old Testament, but as the children grow they should learn about this time of preparation for the coming Messiah. Children like the beautiful stories of the Old Testament. The catechist must help them to see everything in the light of Christ, especially how God prepared mankind step by step, and particularly His Chosen People: the patriarchs, the call of Abraham and the formation of the Chosen People from his family, the liberation from the slavery of Egypt (Exodus) and the solemn Covenant with the Israelites at Mount Sinai, education of the Chosen People in the desert, how God gave them the Holy Land, protected and trained them in the time of the Judges and Kings, how He sent them the prophets in order to purify their cult and call them to repentance. And, as they refused to repent, how He punished them severely (Exile), but at the same time consoled them by the prophets and let them hope more than ever before for the coming Savior.

In order to prepare for Christ, *God stressed in the Old Testament especially* His transcendence (preparing the mystery of the God-man); His oneness (preparing the revelation of the Trinity); His special care for the Chosen People, the Church in preparation, His Covenant with them. Since it is a time of preparation, much is still very imperfect. We encounter many horrible crimes. They illustrate man's need of salvation. Even the greatest religious leaders–Abraham, Moses, David–show great imperfections. The fullness of the times–Christ–had not yet come.

2. Lasting values of the Old Testament

The preparatory character of the Old Testament must not be exaggerated and misinterpreted in the sense that it now has no important lessons for us Christians (See CR, n. 11: "The books of the Old Testament remain permanently valuable.")

Among the lasting values of the Old Testament, the Council stresses above all its presentation of the design of God's plan of salvation and the so-called "types," i.e., happenings and institutions of the Old Testament which foreshadowed happenings and institutions of the New Testament (Adam, Noah, Abraham, Isaac, Joseph, Moses, David, priesthood and sacrifices, etc.). Furthermore, the Old Testament gives us a wonderful presentation of of God's loving and understanding pedagogy in preparing mankind for Christ. In the Old Testament is also found a lively sense of God and a precious treasury of genuine prayer.

God, the inspirer and author of both testaments, wisely arranged that the New Testament be hidden in the Old and the Old made manifest in the New" (CR, n. 16).

Note: In our times almost all catechists who receive a well planned training are given–as they must–special courses on the Old and New Testament. The present exposition of the more outstanding elements of the Christian message is, above all, intended as aid for the systematic study of the content of catechesis. Therefore, in accordance with the GCD, part III, chapter 2, we do not offer here in any detail a study of the particular events of the Old and New Testament and content ourselves to bring to the foreground the basic lines of God's saving plan.

AIDS FOR DISCUSSION AND ASSIMILATION

1. *What do you mean by the Protoevangelium?*
2. *Enumerate the main steps of God in preparing mankind for the Savior.*
3. *What did God specially stress in the Old Testament?*
4. *Enumerate some of the lasting values of the Old Testament.*

> The books of the Old Testament, in accordance with the state of mankind before the time of salvation established by Christ, reveal to all men the knowledge of God and of man and the ways in which God, just and merciful, deals with men. These books, though they also contain some things which are incomplete and temporary, nevertheless show us true divine pedagogy. These same books, then, give expression to a lively sense of God, sound wisdom about human life, and a wonderful treasury of prayers, and in them the mystery of salvation is present in a hidden way (Constitution on Revelation, n. 15).

11

Christ and His Saving Work

Is Christ still relevant to man of today? Why is catechesis on the person and work of Christ so important? Is it enough to present Christ attractively as man and as our brother who shares in everything our human condition?

When the appointed time had come in which God wanted to show His love at its fullest, He sent His Son . . . (see Gal 4:4): By this we enter the inner sanctuary of the Christian message that deals with the person of our Lord and his work among us as Savior, the one sent by God. It is of the greatest importance that our catechesis on Christ be well done.

1. A classical introductory text: Eph 2:1-10

"In the past you were spiritually dead because of your disobedience and sins. [2] At that time you followed the world's evil way; you obeyed the ruler of the spiritual powers in space, the spirit who now controls the people who disobey God. [3] Actually all of us are like them, and lived according to our natural desires, and did whatever suited the wishes of our own bodies and minds. Like everyone else, we too were naturally bound to suffer God's wrath.
[4] "But God's mercy is so abundant, and his love for us so great, [5] that while we were spiritually dead in our disobedience he brought us to life with Christ. It is by God's grace that you have been saved. [6] In our union with Christ he raised us up with him to rule with him in the heavenly world. [7] He did this to demonstrate for all time to come the extraordinary greatness of his grace in love he showed us is Christ Jesus. [8] For it is by God's grace that you have been saved, through faith. It is not your own doing, but God's gift. [9] There is nothing here to boast of, since it is not the result of our own efforts. [10] God

is our Maker, and in our union with Jesus Christ he has created us for a life of good works, which he has already prepared for us to do."

There is first great emphasis upon our hopeless condition without Christ ("dead"). Verse 4 brings out the wonderful opposition ("dramatic aspect") between human malice and impotence on the one hand and God's "exceedingly" great love and power on the other. Verse 5 "vivified us together with Christ": This is the very aim of God's saving plan and action. It is God's free gift (v. 8ff). But after he has vivified us in Christ, God rightly expects the response of new life and action: "walk" in Christ (v. 10).

2. Some basic principles for the catechesis on Christ

a) *What to teach*

Our message concerning Christ should deal harmoniously with his person and with his work. We must answer clearly the question of *who he is:* the God-man. He is the eternal Son of the Father, and since he assumed our human life, he is truly man. "Catechesis ought daily to defend and strengthen belief in the divinity of Jesus Christ, in order that he may be accepted not merely for his admirable human life, but that men might recognize him through his words and signs as God's only begotten Son" (GCD, n. 53).

He came, sent by the father, to accomplish the work the Father had entrusted to him: our salvation. By this, we answer the other important question: *What did he come to do?* After our separation through sin, he had as Savior to unite us again (Eph 1:10). He had to overcome the power of sin and death (Col 1:13ff.) He had to bring us God's life (Jn 1:13ff; Jn 10:10). When we speak of Christ, we never separate these two basic aspects: his divine dignity as the true Son of God, and the saving work he did as man among us and for us.

"There is only one physician, both in body and in spirit, born and unborn, God became man, true life in death; sprung both from Mary and from God, first incapable of suffering and then capable of it, Jesus Christ our Lord" (St. Ignatius to the Ephesians, Enchiridion patristicum, 39; see also GCD, n. 53).

b) *How to teach*

1) *Take time:* Do not hurry; this is the most important part of our message. If necessary, shorten other parts of the Christian message, but reserve enough time to present well what concerns Christ himself.

2) *Present our Lord in a concrete way.* Present the mystery of Christ with the beautiful stories of the gospels. First narrate what happened (event), then show the deeper meaning of this event, the mystery contained in this happening. Learn from good modern commentaries how to explain correctly the narrations of the gospels. What the evangelists are mainly concerned with is not an exact description of events, but a forceful presentation of the message of salvation, the mystery of Christ.

3) *Make a truly attractive presentation* in the deepest sense of the word, winning (with God's grace) the hearts of the audience for an ever deeper and more committed personal love of Christ.

4) *Be faithful in your presentation.* Present Christ as he is shown in the gospels. Above all his spirituality which is characterized by his total dedication to God, his heavenly Father ("Abba, Father").

AIDS FOR DISCUSSION AND ASSIMILATION

1. *What does St. Paul mean by the "fullness of time"?*
2. *What is our main message with regard to the person and work of Christ?*
3. *How are we to speak on Christ?*
4. *How are we to distinguish between the "event" and the "mystery" in our catechesis on Christ?*

This is eternal life: for men to know you, the only true God, and to know Jesus Christ, whom you sent (Jn 17:3).

12

The Mystery of God's "Foolish Love": Incarnation

Was the Incarnation necessary for the salvation of man or had God other ways of salvation? What was the deepest reason for God's coming so close to man through the Incarnation? What do we mean when we speak, with the Bible (1 Cor 1:21-25), about the "foolish" love of God?

Only in the light of man's continuous revolt against God, can we rightly appreciate God's "foolish" (surpassing our understanding) love as we encounter it in the mystery of Incarnation. "The greatest of God's works is the Incarnation of His Son Christ" (GCD, n. 50). In order to understand well the mystery of the Incarnation, we must consider it in the context of God's plan of salvation; that is, in a dynamic and not a static consideration (the mere fact of Incarnation in itself).

1) *What the Incarnation means:* The eternal son of the Father *descended.* He could not lose anything that belonged to him as the Son of God; namely, his divine majesty, power, etc. But, he did not insist upon the honors due to Him as the Son of God. He *assumed* from the Virgin-Mother human life and human existence. He assumed a living human body as his very own in the strictest meaning, and by doing so, he *entered* our human race, not as a stranger coming to us from without, like a "spaceman," but from within, through a human mother, making himself perfectly one of our sinful human race. He *shared* with us his divine riches and accepted our human limitations in order to prove his excessive love: "O wondrous exchange of love." In his "foolish" love, he accepted joyfully what is ours and enriched us unfathomably with his divine riches. He *enabled* us to bring man to his final perfection. He

transformed, sanctified, elevated man and led him back to the Father (Jn 14:2f; Jn 16:28).

2) *The social dimensions of the Incarnation:* Christ came to *unite* himself with us. A most opposite attitude is any kind of separatism, forming oligarchies, exclusive cliques (groups). He came to *share* with us everything that belongs to him. Most opposite: to deprive others of what is theirs. He came to *serve* (Mt 20:28); most opposite: to dominate others. He came to *promote mankind* (a full "yes" to God's plan of creation); most opposite: to exploit others. Christ became man not only to "open again the doors of heaven" for sinful man. He was sent by the Father to bring about a new community of God's children who would commit themselves to fulfill the plan of God the creator and to work in the service of God for the well-being of their brethren already here on earth. (See chapter 6 on Creation.)

3) *Main difference between the former and the "new" presentation:* Formerly, we presented the Incarnation too exclusively as an act of God's mercy. It obviously is. However, it is even more an act of love or friendship, God falling in love with man. As such, it shows God's esteem for man and his world, a personal exchange of self-giving love and permanent and perfect union with the beloved one. *Biblical foundation:* Mt 22:1ff; Eph 5:25ff; Rev 21 and 22.

4) *The consequences of .this presentation* are a most special gratitude for this "foolish" love, a deep, but thoroughly religious self-assurance for man, a revalorization of man and his world, an unshakeable optimism regarding the future of the individual and especially of the human race. This does, of course, not exclude transitory difficulties, and even setbacks, but it means full guarantee of final success and triumph with Christ.

And all of this must be presented as the *manifestation of the Father's love:* "For God so much loved the world" (Jn 3:16). "The kingdom of God may be compared to a king who gave a marriage feast . . . " Mt 22:1ff.

Main titles of Christ: Son of God, Son of Man (Dan 7:13-14), Messiah . . . King . . . Servant of God (Is 52:53), Savior, Lord.

AIDS FOR DISCUSSION AND ASSIMILATION

1. *What does the Incarnation mean?*
2. *How do you distinguish a "static" and "dynamic" consideration of Incarnation?*
3. *What is meant by the social dimensions of Incarnation?*
4. *In what consists the main difference between the former and the "new" presentation of Incarnation?*
5. *What are the main consequences of the new explanation?*

The truth is that only in the mystery of the incarnate Word does the mystery of man take on light. For Adam, the first man, was a figure of Him who was to come, namely, Christ the Lord. Christ, the final Adam, by the revelation of the mystery of the Father and His love, fully reveals man to man himself and makes his supreme calling clear. It is not surprising, then, that in Him all the aforementioned truths find their root and find their crown.

He who is "the image of the invisible God" (Col 1:15), is Himself the perfect man. To the sons of Adam He restores the divine likeness which had been defigured from the first sin onward. Since human nature as He assumed it has been raised up to a divine dignity in our respect too. For by His incarnation the Son of God has united Himself in some fashion with every man. He worked with human hands, He thought with a human mind, acted by human choice, and loved with a human heart. Born of the Virgin Mary, He has truly been made one of us, like us in all things except sin (Constitution on the Church in the Modern World, n. 22).

13

God's Great Instrument in Sending Us His Son: Mary

Did Christ need a human mother if he really wanted to become one of us in the full meaning of the word, a member of the human race? In what sense can and must we say that we owe Jesus to Mary?

When God made the world, he did not invite any angel to assist him. But, when God manifested his love even more abundantly in sending us his Son, he deigned to use as his free human instrument the Blessed Virgin.

1. The unique role of Mary in the mystery of Christ

The meaning of Annunciation is this: God invites the Blessed Virgin into a unique collaboration with him in his plan of salvation; she is to become the mother of the Savior. This is a unique privilege which the Virgin could not "deserve" in any true meaning of the word. But, with the help of God, she could humbly accept this privilege and prepare herself to fulfill her task well. And she accepted it humbly: "Behold the handmaid of the Lord" (Lk 1:38). She was called to physical cooperation with God in the work of Incarnation and was allowed to make her own particular contribution to this great work of God's love. Her personal contribution was free and decisive. It is through his human mother that the Son of the Father entered our human community and became in the strictest meaning, our brother in the flesh, the EMMANUEL, i.e., God-with-us.

The greatness of the Blessed Mother consists in her special place, in her unique role in the mystery of Christ. As free instrument of God, she has given us the Savior, the only source of our salvation. By this, she surpasses all angels and saints. In our official cult, the liturgy, the Church rightly reserves to her a most special place in accordance with her exceptional role in the work of salvation.

Her role in the mystery of Christ is based upon—but not restricted to—her special role in Incarnation. She did not only give us the Redeemer, but is herself most perfectly redeemed—the noblest member of the Mystical Body and the oustanding type of the Church. Because of her role in giving us Christ the Savior in the Incarnation, she also has an important role in communicating to us the fruit of salvation. This is what we mean when we speak about her motherhood in the order of grace.

2. Three basic principles of solid Marian doctrine and devotion

a) *Its doctrinal foundation* in the mystery of Christ. The measure of Marian doctrine and devotion being truly Catholic is the measure of its stressing her special relation to Christ, her absolute dependence upon Christ as her Savior and our Savior. Any kind of doctrine and devotion which is not characterized by this emphatic orientation to Christ necessarily degenerates into wrong sentimentality.

b) *Its filial attitude.* As true Christians, we approach everything with the attitude of Christ (Phil 2:15). One with Christ in the Spirit, we also share in his tender, filial attitude towards his mother. This attitude is ultimately based on his love to the Father who has given him this wonderful mother.

c) *Its necessary balance.* Consider the example of the condiments. All particular devotions have in our spiritual life a similar function as condiments in our food. They make food more tasty and incite our appetite. But they can never, and in no way, substitute for the substantial food. Any Marian devotion, which in fact covers or substitutes for the role of the Father is wrong. The motherhood of Mary must be explained well in order to avoid serious difficulties. In the family we owe our life and its healthy growth in some way even more to mother than to father. Boys especially usually feel closer to mother than to father. In our life with God,

Mary cannot give us her own life at all; she is only instrumental in transmitting God's life to us. In the family father and mother complement one another; we need both. No father has all the qualities of a perfect mother. But God is really in the deepest sense of the word our "Great-Father-Mother" ("ta-fu-mu" a Chinese expression for God). He possesses all qualities of a loving mother in infinite perfection. All the tender love of the Blessed Mother is only some reflection of His infinite love. Vatican II, which gave us the magnificent chapter on the Blessed Mother (chapter 8 in the Constitution on the Church), explicitly warned against any exaggeration in teaching and devotion (CCH, n. 67).

AIDS FOR DISCUSSION AND ASSIMILATION

1. *In what does Mary's unique role in the Mystery of Christ consist?*
2. *What are the main principles of true Marian doctrine and devotion?*
3. *Explain the comparison with the condiments.*
4. *In what sense do we call Mary our mother?*

> This Synod earnestly exhorts theologians and preachers of the divine word that in treating of the unique dignity of the Mother of God, they carefully and equally avoid the falsity of exaggeration on the one hand, and the excess of narrow-mindedness on the other. Pursuing the study of sacred Scripture, the holy Fathers, the doctors, and liturgies of the Church, and under the guidance of the Church's teaching authority, let them rightly explain the offices and privileges of the Blessed Virgin which are always related to Christ, the Source of all truth, sanctity and piety.
>
> Let them painstakingly guard against any word or deed which could lead separated brethren or anyone else into error regarding the true doctrine of the Church (Dogmatic Constitution on the Church, n. 67).

14

The Hidden Life of Our Lord

Would Christ be like us in everything, except sin, if he had not grown, or only grown in his body? What do we learn from the hidden life of Our Lord?

St. Paul speaks emphatically of "the" mystery of Christ and means by this the whole message of salvation centered upon Jesus Christ as the most striking expression of God's saving love. In catechetical and spiritual books we also quite often find the expression "the mysteries" of Christ and by this is meant the particular phases and events of his life as God-man: e.g., incarnation, nativity, epiphany, baptism in the Jordan, etc. Among all these particular "mysteries," the Incarnation is the most fundamental, and the Paschal Mystery is the one by which he "principally achieved his task" as Savior (CL, n. 5). All other mysteries of his hidden and public life must be seen and explained in the light of the Incarnation and the Paschal Mystery (Passion/Resurrection).

1. Meaning and importance of the hidden life of Christ.

By his hidden life, Christ splendidly showed his love, becoming like us in all things but sin (Hb 4:15), taking upon himself the limitations of childhood and growing with us. He "increased in wisdom and in stature, and in favor with God and man" (Lk 2:52). Without true growth, his life would not be truly human.

His hidden life is of special importance to children, and young people in their growth to Christian maturity. From the divine Infant, and not from Moses, Christian children learn the fundamentals of a truly Christian life. They feel close to him who wanted to prove his love by becoming like them, a real and healthy child.

Nevertheless, in the catechesis of children, any exaggerated emphasis on the hidden life of Christ is to be carefully avoided. Healthy children–since they must grow–always look up to adults as their best friends (parents at home), models and leaders. There should be no building up of a particular devotion to the Infant Jesus. Significantly, Mother Church in her liturgy never prays to the Infant Jesus. As in a true dialogue with a person we encounter here and now, the Church addresses itself always to Christ as he is, i.e., to Christ, "who lives and reigns" gloriously with the Father. Gently, but consistently we have to lead children to this kind of prayer.

2. The particular mysteries of the hidden life of Christ.

Matthew and Luke bring in the first two chapters of their gospels very beautiful narratives about the childhood of Jesus. These narratives are not intended as historical reports which give an exact account of facts, but as accounts which have to convey an important message. Compare what you read there with pictures of the Infant Jesus. What counts is the message. For example in the story of the Annunciation: God invited the Virgin; she gave her free and humble response. This exceptional child is in a most special way the gift of God and of a human mother without the intervention of a human father. Nativity: Jesus is the Savior and Shepherd of his people (Messiah, whose type is King David).

AIDS FOR DISCUSSION AND ASSIMILATION

1. *How do you distinguish between the Mystery and the mysteries of Christ?*
2. *Why is the hidden life of Our Lord of special importance for the children?*
3. *Why does the Church in her liturgy never pray to the Infant Jesus?*

> Remember this! Whoever does not receive the Kingdom of God like a child will never enter it (Lk 18:17).

15

The Public Life of Christ: Christ as Teacher

How are we to acquaint our students ever more with the person and teachings of Christ? Was Christ's catechesis a catechesis for children or one for adults? To what kind of people did Christ give his special sympathy and care? With what mentalities did he come to a continuous clash?

In the very first years of elementary grades, we do not introduce much material on the public life of our Lord. But, in the intermediate and upper grades we must acquaint children and adolescents thoroughly with the life of Christ. We must present him to them winningly as the great friend, leader, Savior.

1. Some basic principles for the catechesis on the public life of Christ

a) *Select* the accounts according to the age of your students. To the younger ones, present especially the facts (events). Later on, explain more the teachings of Christ. But do this without separating these two elements too much.

b) *Avoid tiresome repetitions.* If you bring the same story up again in a following year, present it under a new viewpoint with additional new elements.

c) *Show how the work and teaching of Christ form an organic whole.* Both by teaching and by doing what he teaches, he fulfills an important part of his saving task.

d) *Christ's miracles* not only prove his divine mission, but at the same time reveal him as Savior. All miracles have an important message to convey, e.g., the multiplication of the loaves, the healing of the blind, the resuscitation of Lazarus.

e) *Main message of Christ.* In a most simple way, the message can be conveyed to children in the first grades, but later on, it must be ever more deepened: God loves us with the love and care of a true father. We must prove our love for Him most especially by our loving concern for all our brethren—the great Commandment. In later years we must present Christ especially as the great leader, explaining well his great program, the Sermon on the Mount, Mt 5-7 (and his Testament) the sermon after the Last Supper: Jn 13-17.

f) *Build up in your students,* according to their capacity, an ever deeper relationship of personal love and commitment to Christ as their friend, leader, Savior. Stimulate the spirit of prayer, both personal and communal.

g) *In upper grades read whole gospels* with the students, beginning with Luke.

2. Christ—the best and greatest teacher.

Christ compared with Moses, the greatest teacher in the Old Testament (Jn 1:17f).

Christ excelled in a most special way in all the qualities that make a good teacher: *Knowledge:* Coming from God, being the very Son of God (Jn 1:18). *Communication:* The decisive quality of a good teacher which again comprises three elements: *Personal interest* in his students, entrusted to him by his heavenly Father; *consciousness of his mission,* knowing the importance of his message and loving eagerness to convey it to his beloved students; *adaptation to his students,* speaking their language, starting from their situation. His adaptation was the necessary consequence of his love for the Father and for his brethren. Great love always makes one ready to adapt oneself to the beloved person, ready for selfless service (see Mt 20:28).

AIDS FOR DISCUSSION AND ASSIMILATION

1. *Enumerate some of the more important principles of a good catechesis on the public life of Our Lord.*

2. *What is the twofold aim of Christ's wonder?*
3. *How would you, in the simplest way, formulate Christ's message?*
4. *Why do we call Christ the best and greatest teacher?*

What I have spoken to you does not come from myself; no, what I was to say, what I had to speak, was commanded by the Father who sent me, and I know that his commands mean eternal life. And therefore what the Father has told me is what I speak (Jn 12:49 f).

How happy are the poor in spirit;
theirs is the kingdom of heaven.
Happy the gentle;
they shall have the earth for their heritage.
Happy those who mourn:
they shall be comforted.
Happy those who hunger and thirst for what is right:
they shall be satisfied.
Happy the merciful:
they shall have mercy shown them.
Happy the pure in heart:
they shall see God.
Happy the peacemakers:
they shall be called sons of God.
Happy those who are persecuted in the cause of right:
theirs is the kingdom of heaven (Mt 5:3-10).

His teaching made a deep impression on the people because he taught them with authority, and not like their own scribes (Mt 7:28f).

16

The Message of Christ: Gospel and Challenge

Did the Apostles consider their life with Christ primarily as a great experience or as a great sacrifice? What did Christ demand from his disciples? How did Our Lord form them?

The whole message of Christ is characterized by being the *good news of salvation* (gospel), but at the same time a call to repentance.

1. A summary of Christ's message.

St. Mark summarizes very well Our Lord's teaching: "Jesus came into Galilee, preaching the gospel of God, and saying, 'The time is fulfilled, and the kingdom of God is at hand; repent and believe in the gospel' " (Mk 1:14f). What Christ preaches and brings is truly good news, it means the fulfillment of what the best of the Jews had been longing for so long a time, in fact a fulfillment far beyond what they expected. But the necessary condition for entering the Kingdom and enjoying its promises, and even for appreciating this way of fulfillment, is first a thorough change of mind, i.e., repentance.

2. The great program of our Lord—The sermon on the mount, Mt 5-7.

As Matthew presents it in chapters 5-7 of his gospel (see also Lk 6:17-49), it is the work of Matthew, but it presents well the basic ideas which Christ has presented on various occasions.

It is directed above all to his disciples, who did not come just for obtaining some occasional help, but for the right orientation of their lives: "He lifted up his eyes to his disciples, and said" (Lk 6:20). Only an elite will really understand and accept.

He promises blessings and happiness—beatitudes, which must be definitely understood as promises for the life in this world, but only as a beginning. Whoever accepts the gospel will already begin to earn deep joy and peace, although "along with persecutions" (Mk 10:30).

The indispensable condition for sharing this happiness is a thorough change of attitude and life—repentance—as expressed in the eight beatitudes and in the new interpretation of the commandments. They call for complete dedication to God and for radical break with any kind of selfish attitude in our encounter with others.

In sharp opposition to the "righteousness of the Scribes and Pharisees" (Mt 5:20), which must be superseded, Christ puts all the emphasis upon the interior attitude and not on the exterior act. The pure intention decides the value of our action in the eyes of God (Mt 6, 1ff). At the same time Christ makes equally clear that pious words are not enough, man must prove his good will by his actions, "Not everyone who says to me, 'Lord, Lord' shall enter the kingdom of heaven; but he who does the will of my Father in heaven shall enter the kingdom of heaven" (Mt 7:21).

In opposition to the legalistic approach of the Scribes with their complicated system of many clear-cut rules, Christ challenges man to a wholehearted decision for God and His kingdom and complete trust in God (Mt 6:33). This wholehearted unreserved surrender to God necessarily includes a call to perfection (Mt 5:48), not as a perfection already realized in this life, but as the sincere desire of ever more perfect service of God. "Be perfect," means try to become perfect, "as your heavenly Father is perfect."

AIDS FOR DISCUSSION AND ASSIMILATION

1. *Show with Mk 1:14f the main aspects of Christ's message: gospel and challenge.*
2. *Where do we find Christ's "program" presented in the gospels?*
3. *What is the indispensable condition for obtaining the blessings of Christ?*
4. *What is the main difference between the spirituality of Christ and that of the Pharisees?*

17

The Spirituality of Christ

Christ invites us to follow him; what does that really mean? Of all men whoever lived, who was most perfectly under the continuous guidance of the Holy Spirit? To what kind of life did the Spirit of God lead the God-man Jesus Christ?

In all types of catechesis we have to deal diligently with the life of Our Lord, with his hidden and public life. The principal aim of the catechesis is not the particular doctrines and the useful applications to our moral life, but to communicate to our students a deep personal love of Christ, and to "form Christ in them" (Gal 4:19) so that Christ becomes ever more the content and real meaning of their lives. To live a truly Christian life obviously does not mean copying the exterior actions of Christ, but living our own individual life in all its particular situations with the spirit of Christ. How important it is therefore, that the catechist have a very clear understanding and deep appreciation of Christ's spirituality, one with which he is thoroughly imbued himself, and then communicates to his students.

Some basic texts of the Bible which express especially well the spirit of Christ.

Hebr 10:5-7. The will of the Father is the only norm in the conscious human life of Jesus. He was ready to sacrifice himself in order to prove his love.

Lc 2:48-49. The first Word of Christ is related in the Bible. In comparison with his heavenly Father even his wonderful and most tender, beloved mother simply does not count. Behold the perfect devotion to the Blessed Mother as found in the spiritual life of Our Lord and classically expressed in his very first word.

Jn 4:31-34. The will of the Father is his "food." Similar texts abound in John, e.g., 5:30, 6:38 and especially 8:29: "What is pleasing to Him (the Father) I do all the time." The only decisive concern in the whole life of our Lord is to do the will of his Father perfectly, in each situation of his life. Note the typically manly expression of his love in the texts we have just studied. What counts is not the word "love," but its realization in life.

Christ loves deeply his mother, his disciples and all his brothers, but because of the Father who had entrusted them to him. The spirituality of Christ is characterized by the perfect balance of its vertical and horizontal dimension: In order to prove his love to the Father, he dedicates himself to the service of his brethren: "The Father loves me for this: that I lay down my life" (Jn 10:1) as the Good Shepherd "who lays down his life for the sheep" (Jn 10:11).

Jn 14:30-31. The most splendid proof of his love is his blessed Passion: Gethsemane Mt 26:39; Golgotha Jn 19:28-29.

Lk 23:46. His last word a prayer of love. "Father! In your hands I place my spirit!" He said this and died.

In the whole history of man we cannot find any other life so perfectly oriented to God the Father in filial love the life of Christ. Of all men who ever lived, the God-man Jesus Christ was most perfectly under the continuous guidance of the Holy Spirit (see e.g. Lk 3:22; 4:1.14.18). It was the Holy Spirit who "cried" first and most perfectly in the heart of Jesus: "Abba, Father!" (Gal 4:6). His spirituality must be the norm for any authentic Christian life: "Have this mind in you which you find in Jesus Christ" (Phil. 2:5).

As a wonderful recapitulation of his teaching (public life) and as transition to the summit of his life as Savior, the Paschal Mystery, consider Jn 13:1-15. What he taught: Love. Love for the brethren, but motivated by the love of the Father. How he taught: Primarily by doing it, and doing it heroically. By consuming himself for his "students," and this he finally did in his blessed Passion.

AIDS FOR DISCUSSION AND ASSIMILATION

1. *What is meant by the "spirituality" of Christ?*
2. *What are the main characteristics of the interior life of Christ?*

18

The Culmination of Christ's Work as Savior: The Paschal Mystery

Vatican II is striking in its emphasis on the Paschal Mystery and even by the frequent use of the somewhat new and rather different term "Paschal Mystery." What was the intention of the Council in doing so? What are the main differences between the way as the Paschal Mystery is presented in Bible and Liturgy on the one hand and a more devotional approach on the other?

Christ achieved his task as Savior principally by the Paschal Mystery of his blessed passion, resurrection from the dead and glorious ascension (CL, n. 5). This is the summit of the personal work of Christ as Savior, the "Holy of Holies" in the Mystery of Christ. Because of its importance this central part of our Christian message demands special emphasis and a most faithful presentation according to the main expressions of God's Revelation in Bible and liturgy (tradition).

We shall try to understand the true meaning of this central mystery by the analysis of a very important biblical and liturgical text: *Phil 2:5-11,* the epistle of Palm Sunday by which Mother Church every year gives us the orientation for celebrating with her, her most ancient and highest feast, Easter (Holy Week and Octave of Easter by far the greatest festival of Christianity).

Both in Scripture and in the liturgy we find stressed:

1. The necessity of our personal commitment

It needs our personal participation in this mystery. We have to avoid any legalistic presentation such as: "Christ *has paid* to

God the heavenly Father the immense debt which we had contracted by our sin–God thus has received all that he can demand, and we are free of any further obligation." Such legalistic presentation deplorably distorts a decisive truth: after the personal "no" of the sinner, the most holy God can never forgive, as long as the sinner is not willing to change his "no" into a new "yes." Not even the passion of Christ can substitute for our personal conversion and commitment. These are absolutely indispensable. "Have this in mind in you which was also in Jesus Christ" (Phil 2:2-5). We adults are real Christians in so far as we share in His saving obedience. But because of the blessed passion of our Lord we can repent (grace of repentance) and God accepts our repentance.

2. The passover from death to life,

Passion and resurrection form an inseparable unit with the emphasis on the much neglected 15th Station (the resurrection)! Our religion is not a religion of death but of life. At the same time we have to stress that the only way to the resurrection is death. Yet station 12 (death) is transitory, and station 15 (resurrection) is everlasting. Both Scripture and Liturgy are impressive in their emphasis on the resurrection, in presenting the passion in the light of the coming resurrection, and in celebrating the resurrection as the outcome of the "blessed" passion of our Lord.

A good catechesis on the passover of Christ cannot dispense with a solid preparatory study of the great salvific event of the Old Testament, i.e., the passover of the Chosen People from the slavery of Egypt to the freedom and prosperity of the Holy Land, making their Covenant with God in the desert (personal commitment).

3. The love of the Father

The Bible and the Liturgy present the Paschal Mystery above all as the most striking manifestation of the Father's love. "For God loved the world so much that he gave his only Son, so that everyone who believes in him (personal commitment of faith!) may not die but have eternal life. For God did not send his Son into the world to be its Judge, but to be its Savior" (Jn 3:16f). Like Christ himself, St. Paul, the leading catechist in the apostolic Church (Rm 8:32) and St. John (1 Jn 4:8-11), the great friend of Our Lord, see in our salvation through the death of Christ the most convincing proof of Father's love. The same is found in Liturgy. "Father, how wonderful your care for us! How boundless your merciful love! To ransom a slave you gave away your Son" (Exsultet).

Any overemphasis on *satisfaction*—something that God demands and receives—destroys the very meaning of this greatest mystery of God's self-giving love. Among the countless ways of redemption He had at His disposal God has chosen the one which shows most strikingly His "foolish" (1 Cor 1:21-25) love. The right emphasis on God's love in the whole work of redemption does, of course, not rule out other important aspects like that of reparation. But they have to be seen and to be presented in the light of God's redeeming love.

4. The ecclesial aspect of salvation

"From the side of Christ, when he slept the sleep of death upon the cross, there came forth the wondrous sacrament of the whole Church" (CL, n. 5). Christ died and rose, not for himself, but "for us". This "us" means more than just each of us individually. Christ died and rose again in order to reverse the rebellious NO of the "everybody" into a new loving YES and to build up a new family of God's children, one with him in the Holy Spirit. With Vatican II, therefore, we have to see the Church, redeemed mankind, as the main fruit of the Paschal Mystery. The following chapter on the Church must be seen as the extension of this chapter on the Paschal Mystery.

AIDS FOR DISCUSSION AND ASSIMILATION

1. *What do you mean by the Paschal Mystery?*
2. *Why does the Paschal Mystery hold the first place among the mysteries of Christ?*
3. *What are the four main criteria to be stressed in the presentation of the Paschal Mystery?*
4. *Why did Christ die for us? Can he substitute for our personal repentance?*
5. *Why is Resurrection even more important than the Passion of Our Lord?*
6. *What is the place of satisfaction in the Paschal Mystery?*

19

The Main Fruit of the Paschal Mystery: The Church Vivified by the Holy Spirit

In recent years many Catholics lost interest in and loyalty to the Church. What may be the main reasons for this regrettable fact? How should we present the Church to man of today in order to make the Church relevant to him? Preconciliar catechesis did not usually distinguish itself by much emphasis on the role of the Holy Spirit in the work of salvation and in the life of the Church. What may be some of the main reasons for this fact, and what may have been its unfavorable consequences?

"The Church instituted by Christ, had its origin in his death and resurrection" (GCD, n. 65).

1. The new People of God

The Church is the community of God's children who commit themselves in union with Christ to a life of loving obedience in the service of God the Father. They are the true worshipers of God who adore him in spirit and in truth (Jn 4:24). By this, after the rebellion of the "everybody," the Kingdom of God (Father) is established (1 Cor 15:20-28). As soon as we, in union with Jesus Christ, acknowledge God as our Lord, God acknowledges us as his children and as his children we are, of course, his heirs; i.e., sharing in his life and riches, and joint heirs with Christ (cf. Rm 8:14-17).

2. The brotherhood of love

The sincere acceptance of God as our one Lord and Father necessarily includes our mutual acceptance of one another as brothers and sisters. Christ intended to establish his Church as the great brotherhood of love in which all are one in love as he is one with the Father (Jn 17:21-23; 13:34f). It was as the brotherhood of love, truly one in the risen Lord, that the first Christians, immediately after Pentecost, understood and lived their first Christian community (Acts 2:42-47). This also was the great rediscovery of Vatican II with regard to the Church: *"The Church is a communion.* She herself acquired a fuller awareness of that truth in the Second Vatican Council" (GCD, n. 66). "Communion," of course, is not only to be taught, it must be experienced. Without this experience it simply does not exist. The experience has to start in rather small ecclesial communities which, to be sure, must be seen in their living union with the whole Church. Little esoteric groups do not build up, but split the Church.

Preconcilar catechesis used to overemphasize the institutional aspect of the Church. True, its institutional elements must not be denied or unduly minimized. They are, however, not an end in itself, rather they are in the service of the Church as a communion of life, love and all the other spiritual values.

The Church must never be understood as a self-contained community which is just concerned with itself, with its expansion, development and glory. Again it is Vatican II that insisted in *the deep concern of the Church for all mankind.* The largest and most significant document of Vatican II, the Pastoral Consitution on the Church in the Modern World, deals above all with this. The same we find given prominence by other important catechetical documents after the Council (Paul VI, Professio fidei, n. 27; GCD, n. 67). Our commitment as obedient children of God includes as a very important aspect our commitment to work diligently for the realization of God's plan of creation which means the betterment of this world. Vatican II stressed the importance of this "earthly" commitment and explained it in detail (DAL n. 7; CMW, nn. 46-93).

3. The Mystical Body of Christ

This is *the great paschal gift* which together with his individual glorious body (his new, glorious way of existence as man),

Christ has received from his heavenly Father. It is the reward for his filial obedience unto death on the cross. By this we are one in Christ in a very similar way as our whole body is one organism, one reality. Note the great difference between the real unity of a body and the moral unity of a family. But we are, of course, not a body of flesh with Christ, but a "mystical" body. With the word "mystical" we express the "mystery" of this, our real one-ness with Christ. On the one hand, it surpasses the level of our human experience; on the other hand, it is nevertheless real (Jn 15:1-8; 1 Cor 12). As members of the mystical body we must always be at the disposal of Christ our head, and ready to serve the whole body: Jn 15:9, 12-14; 1 Cor 12:26. The law of loving service is the principal law which regulates life and mutual relations within the Christian community.

4. Vivified by the Holy Spirit as its life giving source

Here, in close connection with the teachings of the Church, we have to deal with the Holy Spirit and his important role in the work of redemption. We must learn from the way Sacred Scripture deals with the Holy Spirit. Practically nothing is said in the Old Testament, and very little before Christ promised to send Him (at the Last Supper), and His Epiphany at Pentecost. But, from then on, much is said about His work in the Church and in the faithful, although very little is said about the Holy Spirit Himself.

The Holy Spirit is the source of all activity in the Mystical Body. His function within the Church can be compared metaphorically to the function of the soul within the human body. Like the soul, he unites the members into one living body with Christ as head. That we are really one with Christ, we owe to the Holy Spirit. He also assimilates the particular members to the whole body and lets them grow according to their functions within the body. He activates all members for their harmonious collaboration for the good of the whole body. Thus, the Holy Spirit makes us true disciples and healthy members of Christ and enables us to act in a truly Christian manner.

Of all the activities of the Mystical Body under the vivifying influence of the Holy Spirit, the missionary activity is the most fundamental (Pentecost). In the broad sense, it means all the efforts which aim at incorporating all men into the Mystical Body and forming them to become ever more perfect members and disciples of Christ. The summit of all activity within the Mystical Body is worship, most especially our common worship, Liturgy. (CL, n. 10; see Gal 4:6).

5. Active participation of all members

As in any healthy body, *all members of the Church must actively participate* in the life of the Church. Only babies and mentally sick people are exempted, since they cannot act as children of God, not having the necessary knowledge and freedom. There is no distinction between active and passive members as to contribution and receiving. But the functions are different, and not exchangeable. Even the most important members cannot substitute for the function of the lesser ones in importance, as the heart cannot function for the little finger. With the Council, we must show well and very concretely what these different functions and tasks are in the world of today, using the Constitution on the Church in the Modern World. Then we have to work together for the promotion and christianization of the family, social, civic, economic and cultural life.

6. Authority in the Church

Authority in the Church must be understood as a necessary and brotherly *service* in the Church. Compare this with the skeleton in the human body. The bones are not the most noble members of the body, but are definitely necessary so that the most noble members, like the brain and heart, can work. What ranks first in the Kingdom of God is never power but love. Spiritual power must be understood and exercised as service to promote love (Eph 4:11-15). It must be used exclusively for a better and more efficient service. To abuse it for one's own glory or the domination of others is sinful. Our presentation of spiritual authority must on the one hand avoid any support of spiritual imperialism but on the other hand lead to religious respect and loyal acceptance of the superiors in whom we respect and accept Christ. Christ meant and established his Church as "a people guided by its shepherds, who are in union with the Supreme Pontiff, the Vicar of Christ, and who are under his direction. To them the faithful look with filial love and obedient homage" (GCD, n. 65). "Religious instruction should treat the role of the pope and of the bishops in their office of teaching, sanctifying and governing the Church. It should explain the gift of infallibility in the Church, and the way and manner in which the teaching authority of the Church guides the faithful in truth" (Basic Teachings for Catholic Religious Education, n. 20). All superiors of the "Pilgrim Church" here on earth are like all other members, imperfect, but nevertheless they are God's instruments and representatives and have a special mission to fulfill. More important than the knowledge of juridical details is the building up of the right Christian attitude towards God-given authority. A very balanced presentation is indispensable for its being accepted today, especially by young people.

7. The Pilgrim Church is a Church of sinners and for sinners

Here on earth, the Church is essentially imperfect and unworthy of her divine bridegroom. She needs continuous reform as explicitly stated by Vatican II. The main motive for her reform must be a deep love of Christ. The consciousness of her unworthiness lets the Church look forward to the coming of her divine bridegroom to perfect her and to present her to his heavenly Father as his perfect bride "in splendor, without spot or wrinkle or any such thing" (Eph 5:27). "COME LORD JESUS!" (Rev 22:20).

NOTES: 1) For a timely catechesis it is imperative that the catechist acquaint himself with the teaching of Vatican II on the Church, especially with its two magnificent Constitutions on this subject, the more basic Dogmatic Constitution and the Pastoral Constitution on the Church in the Modern World. In the chapter of GCD on the "More Outstanding Elements of the Christian Message" perhaps no other passages reflect so well the teachings of the Council as those which deal with the Church (GCD, nn. 65-67).

2) The present author is aware of the unusual length of this chapter. In practice it might easily be divided into two units on the Church and the Holy Spirit. But we must always do our best so that those to be catechized see clearly the Paschal Mystery, Church and Holy Spirit as a close unit and, at the same time, as the very core of the Christian message.

AIDS FOR DISCUSSION AND ASSIMILATION

1. *In what sense is the Church the main fruit of the Paschal Mystery?*
2. *Explain the meaning of the "Kingdom of God."*
3. *What does the "Mystical Body" mean? Why do we call the Church the "Body" of Christ? Why "mystical"?*
4. *Explain the role of the Holy Spirit in the Paschal Mystery and in the Church.*
5. *What are the main activities of the Church?*
6. *What is the function of the authority in the Church? Is it necessary? How is it to be exercised?*
7. *Compare the "Pilgrim Church" with the Heavenly Jerusalem.*

THE NEW MAN IN THE SPIRIT

When man accepts the Spirit of Christ, God introduces him to a way of life completely new. It empowers a man to share in God's own life. He is joined to the Father and to Christ in a vital union which not even death can break.

The indwelling Holy Spirit gives a man hope and courage, heals his weakness of soul, enables him to master passion and selfishness. The Spirit prompts man to pursue what is good and to advance in such virtues as charity, joy, peace, patience, kindness, longanimity, humility, fidelity, modesty, continence, and chastity. The presence of the Holy Spirit makes prayer possible and effective.

God's dwelling in the soul is a matchless grace and manifold gift. Its effects have been expressed in many ways. Thus, a sinner is said to be "justified by God" or "given new life by the Holy Spirit," or "given a share in Christ's life in himself," or to receive grace. The root meaning is that a person dies to sin, shares in the divinity of the Son through the Spirit of adoption, and enters into close communion with the Most Holy Trinity (Basic Teachings for Catholic Religious Education, n. 14).

20

God's Innermost Mystery: The Holy Trinity

Why does the Bible tell us much about the role of each Divine Person in the work of salvation, but only little about their communication with one another? Why does Mother Church since the time of the Apostles rarely pray to the Holy Trinity but rather through Christ to the Father in the Holy Spirit?

After having spoken of the three Divine Persons and their role in our salvation, we must teach about the inner unity of their being one God: the Blessed Trinity. The Trinity is not the central doctrine of the Christian religion. The central idea is rather the love of God. But by revealing His love to us, God has revealed Himself as Trinity, manifesting the roles of the Father, the Son and the Holy Spirit in our salvation. This is the reason why we know much more about their personal work in the great story of God's love—the mystery of Christ, our salvation—than about the Blessed Trinity in itself.

1. When to speak of the Blessed Trinity

We should not start the presentation of Christian doctrine with the Blessed Trinity (Sign of the Cross). We present—according to God's "catechism"—first the divine persons according to their role in man's salvation, mentioning the unity with the Father when we speak first of the Son and the Holy Spirit. Only after having presented the promise and coming of the Holy Spirit (Pentecost) can we speak of the Blessed Trinity in a more specific way.

2. What does Holy Trinity mean?

As with any other mystery of Christian Faith, with this mystery too, we must *explain its meaning well,* although we cannot understand its inner possibility; if we do not explain its meaning our message is useless. We must explain that in God there is the Father, the Son and the Holy Spirit, each truly God, and still only one God. We cannot understand how it is possible that God the Father communicates His own love and life to His Son, eternally, yet we proclaim it.

The intimate personal relationship of the divine persons can in no way be "explained" with a triangle (an abstract dead geometrical figure); although the triangle may be used as a suitable symbol after the mystery is explained.

The presentation of the Holy Trinity must always start with the Father, explaining well how God is really and most perfectly Father, sharing His very life with His Son, without losing it. Compare God's perfect fatherhood with the imperfect fatherhood we find here on earth discussing time, sex, partial communication, multiplication, difference. In God, Father and Son have everything in common—all God's life and perfection which is strictly one—and both in one communicate all this, their life and goodness, to a third someone (person), the Holy Spirit. Thus the Father is the only source of Godhead. The Son and the Holy Spirit share perfectly with Him His Godhead, but they have it from the Father, therefore, we say: Christ is God from God (Father). Compare the three "persons" in God with three students in the class.

3. Why did God reveal this innermost Mystery to us?

The free communication of a very personal mystery is a special sign of love and friendship. By revealing this deepest mystery of His own life to us God gave proof of His love. We can only understand very little of it now, but a time will come when we shall enjoy it in heavenly light.

There is much more; this is also *our mystery.* When did Christ, according to the Bible, first speak explicitly of the Holy Trinity? It was when he sent his apostles to baptize (Mt 28:19). In His very great love, God wants to share with us the very same life He shares with the Son and the Holy Spirit. The way of sharing is different, but the life is the same—and He shares it for the sake of love, first in Baptism, and then more intensively, through the other sacraments.

AIDS FOR DISCUSSION AND ASSIMILATION

1. *What is meant by the Holy Trinity?*
2. *What does it mean that the Holy Trinity has been "co-revealed" with the Mystery of Christ?*
3. *When should we speak of the Holy Trinity?*
4. *What must we explain in each mystery of our faith?*
5. *How are we to explain the Holy Trinity?*
6. *Why has God revealed this, His innermost mystery, to us?*

Just as Christ is the center of the history of salvation, so the mystery of God is the center from which this history takes its origin and to which it is ordered as to its last end. The crucified and risen Christ leads men to the Father by sending the Holy Spirit upon the People of God. For this reason the structure of the whole content of catechesis must be theocentric and trinitarian: through Christ, to the Father, in the Spirit. . .

If catechesis lacks these three elements or neglects their close relationship, the Christian message can certainly lose its proper character (General Catechetical Directory, n. 41).

21

The Saving Acts of Christ: The Sacraments

What is the role of the sacraments in the work of redemption? Are they in some way substitutes for a living faith? What would be a good personalistic approach to the sacraments?

Salvation must be thought of not simply as an event of the past, but something that happens among us and with us. It is realized not only, but most especially, in our personal encounter with Christ when we receive the sacraments. Then we receive ever more intensively God's life and, at the same time, commit ourselves to fulfill our role in the salvation of all the world.

Before we deal with the particular sacraments, we present in this introductory chapter some basic principles for the catechesis of the sacraments.

1. Christ himself is 'the' sacrament

Good sacramental catechesis starts with *Christ as the primordial, universal and personal sacrament.* Christ is the visible and efficacious sign of God the Father in communicating to us God's very life; Christ is the sacrament of the Father. It is, however, the whole Christ, head and members, who acts in the sacraments. It is for this reason that the Church "is in some way to be considered the primordial sacrament" (GCD, n. 55). As his "body" by which Christ makes his work of salvation visible and continues it through the centuries, the Church is "the sign and instrument of the intimate union with God" (CCH, n. 1). After having explained, according to the age of the students, the role of Christ and his Church in the work of salvation, we present the seven particular sacraments and, finally, we compare these seven gifts of Christ to one another. It is only then that we can meaningfully work out the definition of a sacrament.

2. The seven sacraments are personal acts of Christ

The seven particular sacraments are the *saving acts of Christ,* and therefore in all sacraments—and not only in the eucharist—there is a *personal encounter with Christ.* "The sacraments are the principal and fundamental actions whereby Jesus Christ unceasingly bestows his Spirit on the faithful" (GCD, n. 55). In baptism, for example, not Father Smith, but Christ himself makes us children of God (see CL, n. 6). We may fittingly use the comparison with a physician to whom we have to go for the requested operation if we really want to be healed. The visible priest could be compared, in some way, with the assistant who lends a hand to the responsible physician.

All seven sacraments are characterized by a *dynamic, real and personal presence of Christ* in the very moment when the sacrament is being conferred, however uniquely in the Eucharist we encounter a permanent presence of Christ. In all sacraments Christ here and now operates in us for our salvation (dynamic), but only in the eucharist even the "thing" used by Christ in his saving action is not just water, oil or mere bread, but truly his body and blood. The water in baptism is and remains mere water.

3. Christ is the main priest in all sacraments

The emphasis must be put on Christ as the main priest and not on his instrument, the ordained priest. But the ordained priest, too, is necessary according to the institution of Christ. Christ wanted to make his saving action within us visible to us and open to our human experience. For this reason he uses visible signs which are meant to represent impressively his interior action and gift. He requires that the sacramental sign be performed by the ordained priest, according to the rules for the different sacraments, in order to let us see and acknowledge Christ himself in his visible and competent representative.

4. All sacraments presuppose faith

As saving encounters, all sacraments "presuppose faith" (CL, n. 59) in the adults: Personal free commitment to Christ as

Savior. "Of themselves the sacraments certainly express the efficacious will of Christ the Savior; but men, on their part, must show sincere will to respond to God's love and mercy" (GCD, n. 56). With the exception of Baptism, sacraments are not to be administered to persons who cannot yet commit themselves sufficiently. The baptism of children, too, requires a true commitment of the responsible educators that the child will be led up to a true personal commitment in due time. As in the whole process of salvation so in the sacraments too, salvation (God's life) cannot be obtained in a mechanical, magical or commercial manner. Sacramental catechesis which favors any kind of ritualism is against the gospel. By ritualism we mean the tendency to substitute some exterior rite for the personal commitment. The sacraments, demonstrate that salvation is the gift and work of God and not of man, but they presuppose the commitment of faith. And faith again presupposes God's saving grace. "Hence, catechesis must concern itself with the acquisition of the proper dispositions, with the stimulation of sincerity and generosity for a worthy reception of the sacraments" (GCD, n. 56).

5. The social dimension of the sacraments

All sacraments have, by their nature, a *social dimension* or community aspect (see CL, n. 59). They should, therefore, be conferred as much as possible in the context of a community celebration.

6. The method of sacramental catechesis

The method of sacramental catechesis has been determined by Christ himself: The visible sign → the invisible gift → gratitude proved by a life according to the sacrament received.

The explanation of the *visible sign* as instituted by Christ, has to lead to the understanding and appreciation of the *interior gift* which Christ personally confers in each sacrament. The true appreciation of this gift will motivate deep gratitude which must be proved by a *life according to the sacrament* received. Only an existential grasp of the sacramental signs and their relevance for human life can lead to the comprehension of their religious meaning in the sacraments. "In the catechesis of the sacraments, therefore, much importance should be placed on the explanation of the signs" (GCD, n. 57).

AIDS FOR DISCUSSION AND ASSIMILATION

1. *What is a sacrament?*
2. *In what sense do we call Christ the primordial, universal and personal sacrament?*
3. *Explain the expressions "saving acts of Christ" and "personal encounter with Christ as Savior."*
4. *What is the difference between the dynamic presence of Christ in all sacraments and his permanent presence in the eucharist?*
5. *What do we mean by ritualism?*
6. *What is the fundamental method of sacramental catechesis?*

The mystery of Christ is continued in the Church, which always enjoys his presence and ministers to him. This is done in a specific way through the signs that Christ instituted, which signify the gift of grace and produce it, and are properly called sacraments (cf. Council of Trent, *Decree on the Sacraments,* Dz.-Sch., 1601).

The Church herself, however, is in some way to be considered the primordial sacrament, since she is not only the People of God but also in Christ a kind of "sign and instrument of the intimate union with God, and of the unity of the entire human race" (LG, 1).

Sacraments are the principal and fundamental actions whereby Jesus Christ unceasingly bestows his Spirit on the faithful, thus making them the holy people which offers itself, in him and with him, as an oblation acceptable to the Father (General Catechetical Directory, n. 55).

22

The Most Basic Sacrament: Baptism

Is the average Christian truly aware of his baptismal commitment? What could be done to make him more aware of it? Is catechesis of youth already sufficiently understood and given as gradual guidance to the full commitment of faith which, in the "normal" case, should precede baptism? Does baptism really make us Christians? In what sense does it and in what sense not?

Among the sacraments, two excel in a special way: baptism as the most basic sacrament and eucharist as the most sublime. Any catechesis of the other sacraments must start with a solid catechesis on baptism and show how what we have received first in baptism is developed more and more in all the other sacraments. As in all the other sacraments, here too, the catechesis must start from the exterior sign, lead on to a deep religious understanding of the interior gift received and finally explain well to what kind of life we commit ourselves by the sacrament.

1. Entrance into the church building

The entrance into the church building signifies our entrance into the Church of Christ by baptism. Through baptism we receive full membership in the Church. Catechumens, who prepare themselves for baptism already belong to the Church in a very similar way as novices belong to a religious community. Protestants who have received valid baptism belong to the Mystical Body of Christ, but do not belong to the Catholic Church as the true visible expression of the Mystical Body.

2. Sign of the cross

The sign of the cross signifies our belonging to Christ as his disciples (catechumens) and as his very members (since the moment of baptism). This living union with Christ lets us share in Christ's own dignity (comparison with the hand of a bishop). Through baptism we become much more holy–deserving of respect–than a chalice. The whole man becomes through baptism a member of Christ, body and soul. Our whole body too, with all its members belongs to Christ as his very own (1 Co 6:15). What great religious respect and care we therefore owe to our body: "You are not your own. You were bought by a high price" (1 Co 6:20).

As members of Christ we must share in his life, go the same way with him, participate in his passover from death to life. "Thus, by baptism men are plunged into the Paschal Mystery of Christ: they die with him, are buried with him and rise with him (cf. Rm 6:4; Eph 2:6; Col 3:1; 2 Ti 2:11); they receive the spirit of adoption as sons, "by virtue of which we cry: Abba, Father" (Rom 8:15) (CL, n. 6).

3. Washing with water

The washing with water–even more expressively: being immersed in and emerging from the water–signifies the forgiveness of sins and receiving of God's own life. Water is a symbol of purification and of new life. Personal sins cannot be forgiven without personal repentance (personal retraction of one's own deliberate "no" to God.). In connection with baptism, we must explain well God's life in us. We should not use the word "grace" too much. We should make it clear that grace is not a godly "thing" but God's very life communicated to us. We should stress how it surpasses by far earthly adoption and even earthly parenthood; how it presupposes God's dynamic, active presence to us. God the heavenly Father not only calls us His children, not only treats us like a good father, but really makes us His children (1 Jn 3:1) by a continuous sharing of life. This communication of life is realized by giving us His Holy Spirit. The special reason why the Father gives us His life is so that we will be incorporated into the Mystical Body of Christ. (See the beautiful passage on the "New Man" in the GCD, n. 60.)

4. Holy words of baptism

The words express relation and dedication to the most Holy Trinity. In baptism, we become members of Christ. God the Father accepts us as His children and gives us His very life through the Holy Spirit who dwells in us. This makes us true brothers of Christ sharing in his Sonship, being "sons in the Son" as Vatican II expresses it. It is through our special union with the glorious Christ (God-man) that we come to such a close, special relationship with each of the Divine Persons.

The words of baptism also express a total dedication to the three-personed God. We might compare this with the consecration of a chalice or of a church by which the chalice or the church building are withdrawn from profane use and dedicated to the special use of the cult. The baptismal consecration constitutes us "holy to God." We should distinguish well between this basic and constitutive consecration which really makes us Christians and additional "devotional" consecrations; for example, to the Immaculate Heart of Mary, which only express our subjective pious attitude and ask for patronage (continuous help and protection). In the strict meaning, we cannot give ourselves to any saint, since once and for all we have been given totally to God: Father, Son and Holy Spirit. But we can ask our heavenly brethren, and especially the Blessed Mother, to intercede for us that we may live ever more perfectly this, our total dedication to God.

5. The baptismal garment and baptismal candle

The baptismal garment and candle remind us of the life to be lived after baptism. "Let us walk in the newness of life." (Rm 6:4). The garment signifies the new dignity as children of God that we have received in baptism. Now after baptism, we have to live up to this dignity and take care never to lose it. The candle signifies our duty as members of Christ: "you are the light of the world" (Mt 5:14). Through our whole life, in word and deed, we must bring light and warmth into the lives of our brethren.

Comparison with Billy. A poor child who has been adopted by a noble family and is now supposed to adapt his whole way of life to the style of this noble family. His older, adoptive brother Jim (Jesus) helps him. Billy has only to be a good friend of Jim and follow his example and he will soon be a perfect member of this family.

St. Paul's program for our life after baptism, "Consider yourselves dead to sin and alive to God in Jesus Christ" (Rm 6:11). Through baptism we have been incorporated into Jesus Christ as his very members and we share in Christ's priestly, prophetic and kingly roles (GCD, n. 57). He wants to use us for his life of filial love, entirely oriented to God, his Father and ours. How horrible if the "hand of Christ" would ever revolt against God again.

AIDS FOR DISCUSSION AND ASSIMILATION

1. *What is the meaning of the entrance into the church building, of the sign of the cross, of the washing with water, of the holy words, of the baptismal garment, and candle?*
2. *Why are we, through baptism, more holy than a chalice?*
3. *Why is personal repentance (contrition) absolutely necessary, in order to obtain the forgiveness of personal sins, even in baptism?*
4. *What is the difference between a constitutive and a devotional consecration?*

By baptism men are plunged into the paschal mystery of Christ: they die with Him, are buried with Him (cf. Rm 6:4; Eph 2:6; Col 3:1; 2 Ti 2:11); they receive the spirit of adoption as sons "by virtue of which we cry: Abba, Father" (Rm 8:15), and thus become true adorers whom the Father seeks (cf. Jn 4:23) (Constitution on Sacred Liturgy, n.6).

23

The Sacraments of Initiation: Baptism, Confirmation, Eucharist

Has Christ instituted his Church primarily as a juridical institution or as the community of God's children who commit themselves to serve and worship Him in spirit and truth? What would be the consequence of an appropriate sacramental initiation into this committed community? Would this not demand that at least one of the sacraments of initiation be given at an age when the recipient is capable of a true and mature commitment? What would this mean for the appropriate age of confirmation?

Through baptism we become members of the Church, but the complete sacramental initiation, since the most ancient times, includes two other sacraments: confirmation and eucharist. These three sacraments form a close unit. In order to understand them well, we must see their special place and function in the initiation of a Christian.

1. Christian initiation through baptism, confirmation and eucharist

In baptism we become members of Christ, we receive the Holy Spirit who unites us to Christ as our head and enables us to act in union with him in the loving service of his Father and our Father in heaven. Thus already, in virtue of baptism, we have the power and the duty to act according to our baptismal commitment as members of Christ and children of God. Considering human nature as it is, in the Church as in any other community, there exists the danger that quite a few members are much more eager to receive from the community than to contribute. In order to stress the importance of our own activity and selfless contribution within the Mystical Body, Christ gave us another sacrament–confirmation–which consecrates and deputes us for our activity as members of Christ giving us a claim to God's special help (grace) that we may fulfill our duty well. Among all our activities, the most necessary and the most sublime is our filial worship together with Christ in the eucharist. This we do most especially and perfectly when in the eucharist we share in the sacrifice of Christ. The eucharist is also the sacrament which nourishes us. In baptism, God gives us His life, making us His very children; in the eucharist, He nourishes us. We can compare this with parents who feed their own children.

The eucharist is the only sacrament of initiation which can and must be often repeated in Christian life. Would that not mean that each eucharist has to deepen and to perfect our initial commitment until it will be consummated by the Lord when he comes again to initiate us into heavenly life? How must we celebrate and participate in the eucharist so that this its objective be truly obtained?

2. Confirmation as the sacrament of Christian activity

Basically, baptism establishes us in power and gives us the duty to act as true Christians. Confirmation is intended to remind us and to strengthen us for this activity as Christians. Because of this psychological function of the sacrament–to remind and to challenge us–the right time for confirmation is, in the case of baptism of adults, instantly after baptism (as was done in the ancient church). In the case of infant baptism we should wait with confirmation until the youngsters understand well their responsibility for personal, active participation in the Church.

Confirmation consecrates us for all our activity within the Mystical Body. A good catechesis before confirmation must present well the whole range of these activities with special emphasis on what is important for them in their particular situation of life, enabling them to commit themselves wholeheartedly to their own share in this activity. We have to avoid any over-emphasis on our task as "soldiers" of Christ. Confirmation consecrates us to be and to act as soldiers of Christ, fighting against all power of darkness within and without us, as his *witnesses* in the midst of the world, his *workmen* in building up the Kingdom of God and as *priests* with him, sharing in his priesthood and worshiping with him.

As the sacrament of Christian activity, confirmation has a special relation to the Holy Spirit who is the source of all authentic activity within the Mystical Body. But this should not let us forget that all sacraments have a close relationship with the Holy Spirit who is more and more intensively communicated in all the sacraments.

AIDS FOR DISCUSSION AND ASSIMILATION

1. *What is the part of baptism, confirmation and eucharist in the sacramental initiation?*
2. *What is the right time for confirmation and why?*
3. *What are the main concerns of our Christian activities?*
4. *Why has confirmation a special relation to the Holy Spirit?*

Confirmation is the sacrament by which those born anew in baptism now receive the seal of the Holy Spirit, the gift of the Father and the Son. Confirmation, as the sealing of the candidate with the Spirit, is linked with the other sacraments of Christian initiation, baptism and the Eucharist. Religious instruction should emphasize the idea of initiation and explain the sealing of the Spirit as preparation for the witness of a mature Christian life, and for the apostolate of living in the world and extending and defending the faith (Basic Teaching for Catholic Religious Education, n. 11).

24

The Eucharist—Promise and Institution

How does the Bible mark the eucharist as the central and most sublime sacrament of the Lord? What do we learn for sacramental catechesis from Christ's promise of the eucharist? What are the more significant features of its institution?

The Bible narrates clearly and in detail how Our Lord promised and instituted the most central and sublime sacrament. The following is not a detailed explanation of these texts, but only some indications for their use in catechesis. This chapter is supposed to prepare for the next one on the eucharist.

1. The promise: Jn 6.

The eucharist is the only sacrament for which we find in the Bible a detailed catechesis presented by the Lord a year before its institution.

The multiplication of the loaves: Jn 6:1-15. The Lord starts his catechesis with a most exciting experience of God's loving care for our life: The gift of wondrous, heavenly bread, like the manna in the desert. In a sacramental catechesis we have to start the explanation of each particular sacrament with conveying an experimental understanding of the visible sign. In the eucharist, the visible sign is food, and more especially food (bread) taken on the occasion of a family meal (community).

Introduction of the eucharistic sermon: Jn 6:26-35. From the experience of that other day Christ directs attention to the even more important food which now (in the fullness of time) the Father wants to give His children as bread of life (in order to give them life): the Father gives food for their life.

First part of the eucharistic talk: Jn 6:35-47. Here Christ speaks directly of faith. Faith is the necessary condition for all sacraments, for the eucharist too. Even the eucharist does not work mechanically or magically.

Second part of the eucharistic sermon: Jn 6:48-60. Here Christ speaks explicitly of the eucharist. We must eat his body and drink his blood in order to have life in us, i.e., God's life which we have received in baptism. Through this life Christ is permanently in us and we in him (Jn 6:57); it must grow into life everlasting.

The reaction to Christ's talk: Jn 6:61-72. Many are scandalized and turn away. Only the true disciples believe. Peter's wonderful profession of faith.

2. The institution of the eucharist: Mt 26:26-29; Mk 14:22-25; Lk 22:14-20; 1 Co 11:23-26.

The exterior setting and preparation: The meal in which the Lord celebrated the first eucharist with the Apostles is clearly described as Paschal Meal. By this the evangelists surely want to stress the inner connection with the Paschal celebration of the Old Testament. Washing of the feet. Importance of interior cleanness and love.

The Expression of Love: "I have greatly desired to eat this passover with you before I suffer: Lk 22:15. Cf Jn 13:1. The eucharist is the great gift of Christ and the Father, the gift of Christ to his Church for the time, until he comes again (cf. 1 Co 11:26).

The Expounding of his Holy Words of institution: What it really is. How to eat and to act. Why they are to do it: "in memory of me." But not a mere commemoration. It is a reenactment proclaiming the "death of the Lord, until he comes" (1 Co 11:26).

AIDS FOR DISCUSSION AND ASSIMILATION:

1. When did Christ promise the eucharist?
2. What did Christ stress in his eucharistic sermon?
3. What do his words of institution mean?

25

The Eucharist— The Central and Most Sublime Sacrament

Although we always gave in catechesis special prominence to the eucharist, preconciliar catechesis on the eucharist was quite often rather superficial. What may have been the main reason for this strange fact? How can our eucharistic catechesis be deepened by learning from its presentation in the Bible and from its celebration in the liturgy?

All seven sacraments are great and important for the Christian life, but the eucharist surpasses them all as the central and most sublime sacrament. In the eucharist we find a very special presence of Our Lord which definitely gives to this sacrament a special dignity. But its preeminence and central position is by no means exclusively due to this special kind of sacramental presence, rather it is basically founded in the fact that the eucharist is the central act of cult in which the Church reenacts the Paschal Mystery of Christ.

What follows are some basic principles on eucharistic doctrine and catechesis. They are intended to spell out the exact meaning and place of the eucharist in the whole plan of salvation and in the life of the Church. We formulate them in such a way that the difference between authentic eucharistic doctrine according to the Bible and the liturgy stand out clearly against a defective "devotional" (sentimental) presentation in the bad sense.

1. The eucharist is the central sacrament

The eucharist is not a catechetical monolith—a single block of stone—but the central sacrament, therefore it needs to be presented in close connection with the rest of the Christian religion, most especially in connection with baptism and the Paschal Mystery. Note the two following principles:

2. The eucharist is the family meal of God's children

The eucharist is not only a visit of Jesus ("Baby Jesus comes for the first time into your heart"), but *heavenly food*—truly the body and blood of Our Lord—which God the Father gives to His children, in order to help them grow in the divine life which they have received in baptism. (Comparison with parents in the family who have to feed their children to whom they have given life.) In order to understand God's intention with regard to the eucharist, it must be understood as the *family meal of God's children.* Its purpose is not only to nourish each of us individually, but to bring the family of God ever closer together in mutual communication, understanding and love. Only in exceptional cases may we receive the eucharist privately. The most fitting time is definitely during holy Mass. Since it is the gift of God the heavenly Father, authentic thanksgiving goes primarily to Him (postcommunion—concluding part of the communion rite.). What God expects from us is more than a short devotional thanksgiving by prayer. He expects us to grow in our life with Christ, to be ever more transformed into another Christ. But this too will not happen magically. It presupposes our sincere commitment, i.e., our generous collaboration. As in family life we receive this most excellent spiritual food (not the only one) in connection with a feast, a celebration of thanksgiving (holy Mass).

3. The eucharist is the reenactment of the whole Paschal Mystery

The eucharist is not only a passive participation in the Passion of Christ, in which we "receive" the fruits of his Passion, but a *true reenactment of the whole Paschal Mystery,* i.e., Last Supper, Passion, Resurrection and Pentecost. In all sacraments we receive the fruits of Our Lord's Passion. This is true in the eucharist too. But in the eucharist we are challenged to reenact (to have an active part) together with our Lord in his Paschal Mystery. The special reason why our Lord instituted the eucharist was not only to provide us, in the name of his heavenly Father, with heavenly food for our life in God, but also to enable his beloved Bride (the Church) to share with him, his loving offering of himself to God, his and our Father.

In order to fulfill the intention of Christ when he instituted the eucharist, it is not enough that the priest privately celebrate Mass for his flock and give them holy Communion. By this we do not say that private Masses have no value, we only stress the necessity of the active and personal participation of the people. The special function of the ordained priest is to represent visibly and efficiently Christ the High Priest in the midst of his flock. The ordained priest is necessary for celebrating Mass validly. By this Christ wants to make clear that Mass is our action with him, visibly represented by his priest. But he wants to offer with us, and not just for us. More than in any other liturgical act of the Church, it is in the eucharist that "full, conscious and active participation (of the faithful) is demanded by the very nature of the liturgy" (CL, n. 14).

a) *Reenactment of the Last Supper.* "Do this in memory of me." "Take this, all of you and eat (drink) it." By only watching what the priest is doing, we do not fulfill the testament of Christ. The main fruit of the eucharist (Mass) which God has intended for us can only be obtained by receiving holy Communion. Spiritual Communion during holy Mass—supposing that we can actually receive communion—is a contradiction. Compare with taking food in the family.

b) *Reenactment of the Passion.* The Passion, that is, the loving obedience of Christ on Calvary, is in fact reenacted by us when we offer ourselves with Christ, offering his body and blood as a symbol of our sincere commitment to participate in his saving obedience.

The *Sacrifice of the Cross* and that *of the Altar* are not one and the same sacrifice by identity, but by their mutual correlation and complementarity. In order to explain this well we must show their correlation, and what they have in common, but also how they differ. The main priest in both is Christ, but on the cross it is the individual Christ and on the altar is the mystical Christ; the host on Calvary is the individual Christ and on the altar his body and blood stands for us who commit ourselves to the same perfect love and service of God; the principal aim of any sacrifice is always adoration (acknowledging God as the Lord and our total dependence upon Him). But on calvary it is the adoration of repentant mankind (Christ as our Leader retracting our "no") and on the altar it is the adoration of thanksgiving, acknowledging the God of boundless love which we have experienced in the redemption through Christ. Therefore, there is also a great difference in the way of celebration. On the cross we find torments and shedding of blood to express repentance and reparation, and in the eucharist, a joyful celebration of thanksgiving.

c) *Reenactment of Resurrection and Pentecost.* The main reward and paschal gift of the Father to His Son is the Mystical Body vivified by the Holy Spirit; in the sacrifice of the Mass we join in the saving obedience of the Son. It is for this reason that the Father gives us in holy Communion more abundantly His life and His Spirit. In the same measure as we join through our personal commitment during the sacrifice in the loving obedience of Christ, we grow through holy Communion in our union with the Risen Christ and look with confidence to our final union with him and to the final communication of the Holy Spirit in the eternal paschal feast. But already, after each holy Mass, Christ sends us to continue his saving work here on earth as he sent the Apostles at Pentecost filled with the Holy Spirit.

4. The eucharist is the anticipation of the heavenly Pasch

The eucharist does not just look back to the past (as reenactment), but at the same time *points also to the future.* Each Mass is by its nature a prelude and anticipation of the eternal paschal feast, when in final and perfect union with Christ, we shall praise forever the Father's triumphant love. Each holy Communion is a pledge of our future resurrection with Christ (Jn 6:55) and should make us long more for the heavenly and everlasting union with the triune God, again through Christ, the God-man, our head and Savior.

5. The eucharist is the main act of common worship

The eucharist is not just an individual obligation of each Christian, but above all *our basic act of common worship,* the cult of the redeemed people of God, in the time of our pilgrimage, our solemn renewal of the New Covenant. In holy Mass the Church joins and ratifies the Covenant which Christ in our name has made on Calvary. In holy Mass we commit ourselves to live in the world as the "holy" people of God, as the "sacrament of the World." Especially Sunday Mass must be understood and celebrated as the renewal of our baptismal commitment in common. Each of us commits himself not only for himself, but to contribute as far as he can that the community live up ever more perfectly to its Christian commitment. We should never forget that this Christian commitment includes as an essential part our contribution to build up a better world according to God's plan of creation.

6. The eucharist is the summit and center of the Christian life

Thus the eucharist is not just one among many good religious practices (like the rosary, holy hour, etc.), but the *source, center, and summit of the Christian life,* and must be presented as such in all forms of catechesis.

Whoever presents well holy Mass, necessarily presents well the very core of Christianity; who understands well holy Mass understands well what the Christian religion really means; whoever lives according to his commitment in holy Mass, lives a truly Christian life.

AIDS FOR DISCUSSION AND ASSIMILATION

1. *What is the main reason for the preeminence and central position of the eucharist among all sacraments?*
2. *Who gives us the eucharist? What does the Heavenly Father give us in the eucharist and why?*
3. *What is the special connection between the eucharist and baptism? Give two ways this connection is seen.*
4. *What is the difference between a mere commemoration and a true reenactment?*
5. *How is the eucharist the "reenactment" of the whole Paschal Mystery: Last Supper, Passion, Resurrection and Pentecost?*
6. *What have the sacrifice of the cross and Mass in common, and how do they differ?*

7. *What is wrong with spiritual communion during holy Mass?*
8. *How is holy Mass the renewal of the New Covenant?*
9. *How is holy Mass the source, center and summit of the Christian life?*

The other sacraments, as well as every ministry of the Church and every work of the apostolate, are linked with the holy eucharist and are directed toward it. For the most blessed eucharist contains the Church's entire spiritual wealth, that is, Christ Himself, our Passover and living bread. Through His very flesh, made vital and vitalizing by the Holy Spirit, He offers life to men. They are thereby invited and led to offer themselves, their labors, and all created things together with Him.

No Christian community can be built up unless it has its basis and center in the celebration of the most holy eucharist. Here, therefore, all education in the spirit of community must originate. If this celebration is to be sincere and thorough, it must lead to various works of charity and mutual help, as well as to missionary activity and to different forms of Christian witness.

Moreover, by charity, prayer, example, and works of penance, the Church community exercises a true motherhood toward souls who are to be led to Christ. For this community constitutes an effective instrument by which the path to Christ and to His Church is pointed out and made smooth for unbelievers, and by which the faithful are aroused, nourished, and strengthened for spiritual combat (Decree on the Ministry of Priests, nn.5.6).

26

The Great Drama of Holy Mass

The best eucharistic catechesis works in vain if the eucharist is not appropriately celebrated. What would be the basic principles for such an appropriate celebration? How must the celebration of the eucharist be adapted to the particular situation of the participants?

In comparing holy Mass with a drama we stress the aspect of a community action which represents some important event; in our case a "re-presentation" in the strict meaning, a true reenactment of the work of Redemption. In this drama we are supposed to participate as actors and not as mere spectators. Salvation is not just narrated, played, but "acted" in reality.

Holy Mass is a drama in *three acts* with an introduction (entrance rite) and a short conclusion. It is impossible to act well in this drama without understanding its very meaning and without being interiorly committed to its special aim.

The Entrance Rite: Preparing ourselves for our action together with Christ. Special dynamic (active) presence of Christ during the whole Mass. Joyfully we greet him when he enters, visibly represented in his ordained priest. Humbly we admit that we are unworthy of him, since we are sinners (cf. Lk 5:8). Christ cleanses us in a way similar to his preparing the Apostles by washing their feet. The Gloria, when recited (sung), expresses well the special aim of the whole action: Giving joyful praise to the Father · through Christ in the Holy Spirit. The Collect is the summit and priestly conclusion of the entrance rite, Christ takes over his role through the priest. On feast days the Collect formulates the special meaning of the feast and asks for God's grace accordingly.

1. The readings: The Liturgy of the Word—the first act of the drama

Here God speaks to us, we listen with loving interest and true eagerness to accept God's message for our life. This kind of listening is true worship. Gradation of the readings: Prophets (O.T.)—Apostles—Christ (Gospel). The intermediate song should foster reflection upon and response to the readings. The homily expresses Catholic use of the Bible under the guidance of Mother Church. It applies the readings to our life here and now, and should prepare us for the following eucharistic celebration. In the Creed, when recited, we give our response of faith to God's whole revelation. The particular readings of the day must be understood as representing the whole and must be explained and accepted accordingly.

The Prayer of the Faithful concludes the first act of holy Mass and introduces the second. To the Word of God we give first the answer of our word, and then, in the second act, the answer of action. Our petitions significantly are introduced and concluded by the priest who represents Christ, our Mediator. They should express in a truly Christian manner our concrete spiritual and earthly needs: The cry of the Pilgrim Church in the trials of her pilgrimage.

2. The thanksgiving—the second act of the drama

We answer to God's clear offer of love proclaimed in the readings by giving ourselves with our gifts. They stand for us.

Bringing and presenting our gift—the Offertory. This is still a preparatory action. The aim of the offertory is to emphasize our (the people's) part in the following Eucharistic action. The gifts stand for the people of God. With the gifts we bring ourselves to the altar. By presenting our gifts for the sacrifice we express our interior readiness to be changed and to be offered to God by our High Priest Jesus Christ. In the offertory nothing is "offered" but only brought and presented, i.e., finally prepared for the following offering.

With the Preface begins our great thanksgiving. It is the first and very important part, since it expresses especially well both the idea of thanksgiving—three times emphatically asserted—and the people's active part in this thanksgiving (introductory dialogue and Sanctus).

The Eucharistic Prayer in which Christ, through the words of his ordained priest, changes our gifts into his body and blood, and in union with Christ we offer them to God our heavenly Father. This definitely is our action and our prayer: *We offer,* we as the people of God, one with Christ our Savior and divine brother in the unity of the Holy Spirit. The active part of the people in this prayer-action is now very impressively brought out by acclamation immediately after the consecration. It emphatically asserts the central mystery of our faith—the Paschal Mystery—as reenacted here and now in holy Mass, and prepared for the coming of Our Lord in glory. The eucharistic prayer concludes with the great Doxology (prayer of praise) spelling out for a last time the innermost meaning of eucharistic prayer—action. The *solemn Amen* of the people expresses once again the people's active part in this prayer—action with Christ.

3. The holy meal—the third act of the drama

Here God feeds his beloved children: loving union with God the Father and sharing in his life and glory (resurrection) is the main fruit of our participation in the sacrifice of Christ. The Our Father must be understood as saying grace for the coming meal. The Sign of Peace reminds us of the necessary condition for true union with God. Whoever is not disposed to give the sign of peace with a sincere heart to all his brethren is not disposed to receive holy Communion well. He would do better to stay away.

With the words, "This is the Lamb of God," and then again with "the Body of Christ," the priest challenges our faith. With our "Amen" we express our sacramental commitment. Like any other sacrament, the eucharist, too, is not a magic; it works salvation in the degree to which we commit ourselves in faith.

The Postcommunion is the priestly conclusion of the communion rite. After we have been nourished by God our Father, we ask that his heavenly gift may effect its results in our Christian life. There we must prove the depth of our Eucharistic commitment with the help of God's grace.

The *whole celebration ends* with our being sent to realize in our lives what we have promised again in holy Mass. For this we receive the final blessing. Singing, we leave, bringing to everyone the peace and love and joy of Christ.

AIDS FOR DISCUSSION AND ASSIMILATION

1. *Why do we call holy Mass a "drama"?*
2. *What is the structure (main parts) of holy Mass?*
3. *What is the meaning of each of these parts?*
4. *When does each of these parts start and end?*

Mother Church earnestly desires that all faithful be led to that full, conscious, and active participation in liturgical celebrations which is demanded by the very nature of the liturgy. Such participation by the Christian people as "a chosen race, a royal priesthood, a holy nation, a purchased people" (1 P 2:9; cf. 2:4-5), is their right and duty by reason of their baptism.

In the restoration and promotion of the sacred liturgy, this full and active participation by all the people is the aim to be considered before all else; for it is the primary and indispensable source from which the faithful are to derive the true Christian spirit. . . . Therefore, through the needed program of instruction, pastors of souls must zealously strive to achieve it in all their pastoral work.

Yet it would be futile to entertain any hopes of realizing this goal unless the pastors themselves, to begin with, become thoroughly penetrated with the spirit and power of the liturgy, and become masters of it (Constitution on Sacred Liturgy, n,14).

27

The Christian Life to Which We Commit Ourselves in the Sacraments of Initiation

In what consists finally the Christian life we are supposed to live? Is it primarily the careful fulfillment of a set of rules, or is it, above all, a life which grows out of our basic attitudes of faith and love? Can prayer substitute for action, or action substitute for prayer? What follows from the answer to the preceding question for an authentic Christian education?

In the sacraments of initiation, we commit ourselves once and for all to a life in union with Christ. What does this life really mean? We consider here the Christian life not as in the last chapters as God's gift of Himself to us, but *our own activity* according to our new union with God—how we have to act as His beloved children.

In order to live this new life well and constantly, we need God's help. We call it *actual grace,* i.e., God's help for our action. What counts is not the word, but the deep humble conviction that we need God's continuous help in order to serve him well. God is always ready to help us, but we must ask him. We must prove by our whole attitude that we do not trust in ourselves. The trust in God does, of course, in no way dispense us from making resolute efforts to serve Him well. How God's help and our own free will in fact work together, is one of the great mysteries which we can never fully explain.

1. Some basic aspects of the Christian life

A true Christian life is much more than a mere keeping of many rules. In order to help our brethren to live as true Christians, it is not enough to teach them a multitude of rules—"you must." Much more important is to help them to understand and to appreciate ever more the basic call of a Christian and the basic attitudes which this call necessarily implies. The Christian life is by its nature:

a) *A life of faith.* Rm 1:17. This means a life which in its various decisions is ruled by faith. "Yes, Father, and always, yes", fulfilling God's will in every situation of our life, as far as we understand it. In other words, "lived" faith (living faith).

b) *A life of love.* 1 Jn 4:16. "We believe the love God has for us." To believe God's love means answering it by love for love. Therefore, the basic and all-embracing commandment of love (Mt 22:34-40).

c) *A life with Christ.* Gal 4:19; Eph 4:11-15. God has loved us as his very children. We answer by filial love. The model of this love is Christ. In our Christian life we are not only to imitate Christ as we may admire and imitate some hero. We are supposed to become one with him and to live and love with him. Our life is truly Christian as far as it expresses in all its particular phases the very mind (spirituality) of Christ. See chapter 7.

d) *A life in the Holy Spirit.* It is the Holy Spirit who makes us one with Christ and lets us live "in the spirit of Christ". "For those who are led by God's Spirit are the sons of God. For the Spirit God has given you does not make you a slave and cause you to be afraid; instead he makes you God's sons, and by the Spirit's power we cry to God, 'Father! my Father!' (Rm 8:14f). Authentic Christian life is characterized by this joyful awareness of God's life and love in us. The more we open ourselves to the influence of the Holy Spirit, the more abundantly He produces in us His fruits: Love, joy, peace, patience, kindness, goodness, faithfulness, humility and selfcontrol" (Gal 5:22f). Genuine Christian life is by its very nature dynamic, optimistic, generous, initiative and exuberant, but never without the necessary "selfcontrol" as explicitly stressed by the Apostle (Gal 5:23; see also Gal 5:13).

e) *A life of conversion.* Rm 8:28ff. What God expects of us is that we let ourselves be transformed into the image of Christ. We have to express Christ ever more perfectly in our whole life. This means our conversion into another Christ, not by a momentary conversion, but by an *ongoing process* of conversion which will end at our death.

2. The main components of a Christian life: Prayer and action.

As man is composed of body and soul, Christian life is composed of prayer and action. Both elements are necessary and must be vitally united. Prayer is like the soul; action is like the body which needs to be animated by prayer. What counts is not the length of prayer but its quality and its depth in penetrating and directing our activity.

AIDS FOR DISCUSSION AND ASSIMILATION

1. *What is the inner relation between the Christian life and God's life in us?*
2. *What is meant by actual grace?*
3. *What are the four main aspects of the Christian life?*
4. *What are the two main parts of the Christian life?*
5. *Explain the comparison of prayer and action with body and soul in man.*

Catechesis performs the function of disposing men to receive the action of the Holy Spirit and to deepen their conversion. It does this through the word, to which are joined the witness of life and prayer (General Catechetical Directory, n. 22).

28

Our Filial Dialogue with God: Prayer

Why do people usually pray? Why do many people nowadays, especially youngsters, stop praying? How could we make prayer meaningful, important and attractive to them?

Countless defects in prayer originate from errors about the very nature of prayer.

1. What does prayer really mean?

In every true friendship, we find as an indispensable element a dialogue of love. The persons who love each other with marked eagerness engage in mutual communication by which they mutually express their admiration, their love, their loyalty. Provided that we really love God, we must have this direct personal communication with Him as our Lord and Father. To God's greatness, we answer by profound adoration, acknowledging and admiring His Majesty. To God's love we answer by love and a desire for ever more intimate union with Him. It is this dialogue of our heart with God which we call prayer.

In our dialogue with God, *we do not need words* and exterior gestures. God knows perfectly what, deep in our heart, we want to tell him. He always understands our true meaning and desire, even if we cannot express clearly ourselves by words and exterior signs. But quite often, it helps us to use words, to speak them reverently and to express our reverence and love by gestures and actions. In prayer education we can never stress enough that *only the heart can pray:* hands and mouth may help the heart in prayer, but they can never pray without the heart.

By the word "heart," we mean here *man's willful decision* for and dedication to God. It is always by our free loving commitment to God that we pray. The intellect alone cannot pray. It can speculate about God; it can motivate and help prayer. But, it is our free will that alone commits itself to God in loving adoration. By this it is clear that mere pious feelings too, are not prayer. They may help us very much in our communication with God, but what counts in prayer is never our feeling, but the sincerity and depth of our commitment to God.

Prayer is *communication with God.* Prayer in the full meaning of the word is our listening to and speaking with God Himself. Prayer to the saints is good and helpful, as far as it fosters our dialogue with God; it has a preparatory function. The biblical meaning of prayer is dialogue with God. We should have another word for speaking with the saints since it is essentially different and must be distinguished from prayer in its full meaning. Here too, the official prayer of the Church, the liturgy, must be the norm for our private prayer. The Church admires and loves the saints, and thinks of them as her greatest sons and daughters and models of Christian life, the first fruits of redemption. But only a very small part of liturgical prayer goes to the saints and definitely never stops with any saint. Prayer to any saint is always followed by prayer to God Himself. The Church prays much more with the saints than to the saints.

2. Two instructions of Our Lord on prayer

a) *Christ speaking with the Samaritan Woman:* Jn 4:21-24

Christ's first instruction on prayer which we find in the Bible is his colloquy with a woman who was a sinner, "heretic and schismatic." In spite of all that, she is supposed to understand these basic principles of the "new" messianic worship. Its main characteristics are: It is *filial worship.* Now God has revealed Himself as our Father through His Son. It is *worship in spirit and truth.* What counts is the interior attitude, not the exteriors (place, gestures, formulas, time, etc.). It requires full sincerity with the exclusion of any kind of hypocrisy.

b) *Christ on prayer in his great program:* Mt 6:5-15.

At the heart of the Sermon on the Mount, Christ's teachings on prayer are recorded. The following points are strikingly clear from this short statement on prayer:

1) Christian prayer *ascends to God our Father.* Half of the text is a model prayer, the Our Father. In the rest, he again speaks 5 times explicitly about the Father and nobody else.

2) *It must be sincere* excluding any kind of hypocrisy, i.e., to pray in order to be seen and admired by men. What counts in prayer is the purity of the motive, not the exterior posture, length, etc.

3) *It must be characterized by simplicity and depth of faith.* "Believing" in a multitude of words is called a "pagan" attitude. We must speak to God with the simplicity and trust of a child; the Father knows all our needs before we open our mouth. What He expects from us is in no way a detailed exposition of our needs and, even less, of the particular way we want to be helped, but the true manifestation of our full dependence upon Him, of our confidence in Him.

4) *The use of words and set formulas* of prayer is clearly approved and even recommended by the magnificent formula Jesus gives us with the Our Father. The *main characteristics* of this great prayer: we approach God as Father; we pray, united as brothers. Our sincere commitment to this brotherly union is the condition of being accepted by God as His very children. The whole prayer is an expression of filial love and concern primarily with what belongs to God. But significantly, this is formulated as petitions. It is short and substantial.

5) *Prayer must be linked up with our life.* If we are not ready to live according to our prayer, God is not ready to listen to it.

3. Prayer in union with Christ

Christ has brought us a wonderful new way of prayer. Christ came to renew mankind; he established a new community of children of God. Further, he is the head of the Mystical Body. Within the Mystical Body, our most noble and most basic activity in union with him is our common worship by which we express our loving adoration, our gratitude and our readiness to prove our love by our faithful service. Christ not only told us we should pray in his name (Jn 16:23f), but promised us that he will pray with us whenever we pray together (Mt 18:19f). *The more we unite ourselves with Christ in our prayer and let him take the lead, the more our prayer is truly and fully Christian.* It finds its most noble expression in the official prayer of the Church—her Liturgy. But here, too, what finally counts is not our *exterior participation* in the worship of the Christian community, but our sincere and deep commitment to the whole Christ (head and members) and our union with him by faith and love. Precisely by this, our *interior union* with Christ, our prayer becomes prayer in *the Holy Spirit* who enables us to pray, "Abba, Father" (Gal 4:6).

AIDS FOR DISCUSSION AND ASSIMILATION

1. *What is prayer?*
2. *What is the value and function of prayer to the saints?*
3. *What are the main characteristics of "messianic" worship?*
4. *What makes our prayer truly "Christian"?*
5. *What is liturgy?*
6. *What is the value of private and public prayer?*

> The People of God have always been a praying people. Religious educators then, who are mature in the faith and faithful to this tradition, will teach prayer. This teaching will take place through experiences of prayer, through the example of prayer, and through the learning of common prayers. Religious education, at home or in the classroom, given by a teacher who values prayer, will provide both the instruction and the experience. . . .
>
> By instruction in prayer, through all levels of religious education, the learner is gradually led on to a more mature prayer—to meditation, contemplation, and union with God (Basic Teaching for Catholic Religious Education, p. 3).

29

Christian Action

Is every good action already "Christian" in the strict meaning of the word? What ultimately makes our action truly "Christian"? Why did God give commandments if he made us free? Are His commandments a restriction or an aid to our freedom?

Good Christian prayer, by its very nature, leads to action according to God's will. What does God expect us to do? How? Why?

1. What are we supposed to do?

When we put the question, what are we to do, we should *not run precipitately to the commandments.* The commandments tell us what we "must" do. Understanding Christian life as a life of friendship with God, we should ask above all what is it that we can do in order to prove our love and to grow in our friendship with God. Compare this with friendship here on earth.

We Christians are the members of Christ at each moment, we must be at his disposition. "You are not your own; you were bought at a high price." (1 Cor 6:20). Does this not mean that the true Christian at any moment of decision should ask himself what Christ, his Lord in this very situation wants him to do? This question, of course, supposes that we are sufficiently acquainted with the mind of Christ through the gospels and that we are generous enough to follow the direction of Christ. In the vast majority of situations in life, it is quite obvious *what Christ here and now would advise us to do.* What is lacking is not knowledge, but the necessary interest and generosity. In cases of more difficult decisions the true Christian, according to the importance of the matter, is eager to seek the will of God. God manifests his will above all through the directions of our superiors and—in fact even more—through the situation and happenings around us. No one can find the will of God without paying attention to the "signs" of the times (Mt 16:3).

Although we should as true Christians keep ourselves open for the wishes of God, we must always put first things first, and therefore at least observe faithfully the *commandments.* They tell us what we are obliged to do. We have to present them well in Christian catechesis. Christ himself speaks clearly regarding the commandments. He makes it unmistakeably clear that there is finally only one commandment, the great commandment of love, which includes all the rest (Mt 22:40). Not that we are allowed to minimize the particular commandments, but we must see and explain them as the more important practical applications of the one commandment of love. Deliberate concentration upon the one commandment of love leads to a *personalistic approach* to Christian morality; any over-emphasis on the multitude of commandments leads to a *legalistic approach* in which the particular rule easily becomes an end in itself.

Like any other part of our message, the commandments must be presented as a part of Christ's "gospel" and not as a heavy but inevitable burden. It is not enough to emphasize that a life according to the commandments "finally" brings great reward in heaven; it must make human life here on earth truly great and happy. Especially in the catechesis of adolescents and adults we have to show well how in each particular commandment, God, because of his loving concern for us, *fosters and protects some important good of human life.*

In the *first three commandments* God fosters and protects the right personal attitude of man towards God. It is the very basis of our friendship with God and therefore of our own true greatness and happiness.

In the *fourth commandment* God fosters and protects the right communication of superiors and subjects, an indispensable condition of meaningful community life and community development. This commandment is by no means a protection of lazy and irresponsible superiors—just the opposite.

The *fifth commandment protects* life, God's most basic gift to us.

The *sixth commandment* fosters and protects committed love, the responsible transmission of human life, and the necessary conditions for a healthy growth of youth within a community of deep and stable love.

The *seventh commandment* secures the necessary conditions for human progress in this material world (organized work and the just distribution of material goods) and protects the fruits of our work.

The *eighth commandment* secures necessary conditions of community life and mutual communication: truth and good reputation.

The *last two commandments* inculcate the importance of the right inner attitude. The moral value of man does not depend upon his exterior actions, but upon his interior attitude towards God and his fellowmen.

Although we have to show as clearly as we can in our teaching what God expects us to do, there should always be due emphasis upon the "how" and "why" of Christian action.

2. How true Christians are supposed to act

The interior attitude is the most characteristic aspect of good Christian life. We find in the public life of Christ the continuous uncompromising fight of Our Lord against the wrong piety of the religious leaders in his time, the Scribes and Pharisees. The Lord does not deny that they did much; he criticized them for doing it wrongly, with a wrong interior attitude which spoiled the whole. What are the main differences between *authentic Christian attitude* and *pharisaical attitude?*

Christ puts *first things first,* the Pharisee is lost in many little things, and neglects the more important ones; "straining out a gnat and swallowing a camel" (Mt 23:24). Christ stresses *the interior;* the Pharisee is over-concerned with the exterior (Mt 23:26). Christ stresses *quality,* the Pharisee, quantity. For Christ religion means humble and loving *self-surrender* to God, giving himself; for the Pharisee religion means "business" with God, giving things, and receiving things, and reserving himself.

3. The "why" of authentic Christian action

The true value of our actions depends above all upon the *intention* we have when we act. An action is truly Christian, i.e., accepted by Christ as his own—the action of His member—as far as it is rooted in, motivated by, and directed by *faith, hope and charity.* We do not say that all other actions are sinful—this would be very wrong—we only say all other actions are not really "Christian."

Some basic principles with regard to the *"good intention."*

a) The good intention, i.e., the conscious orientation of our activity to its very goal in the light of faith, needs to be *renewed.*

b) In the renewal of our good intention the *depth of the act* is much more important than the number of its repetitions. Mechanical repetitions do not count.

c) The classical occasion for renewing our thorough orientation to God in Jesus Christ is holy *Mass.* Other forms of prayer, too, can be very helpful, e.g. aspirations.

d) Good and meaningful *natural motivations* are not to be substituted for by supernatural motivations, but to be accepted in the light of faith. (Example of sport.)

e) The *essential good intention* in each particular activity is always that we want to do it to obtain the result which God wants us to obtain by this very action. Examples from our daily life: eating, sleeping, studying, etc. Additional intentions are secondary; they can more hinder than help. The main question is always: What does God my heavenly Father want me to do here and now, and why? Avoid artificial good intentions, e.g., to say three Our Fathers in honor of the Immaculate Heart of Mary for the souls in Purgatory.

AIDS FOR DISCUSSION AND ASSIMILATION

1. *What is the most significant question in a life of true love?*
2. *What is the relation of the particular commandments with the basic commandment of love?*
3. *What do you understand by a legalistic and by a personalistic approach to moral life?*
4. *What is the respective particular good which God intends to foster and to protect in each commandment?*
5. *What are the main differences between Christian and pharisaical attitude?*
6. *What is a good intention? How do you distinguish the essential ("immanent") good intention from additional good intentions?*

30

Meaning and Sacrament of Christian Repentance

Was God fully aware of man's weakness when he invited man to friendship with Himself? In what sense is the sacrament of Penance the most "human" sacrament? Why does it reveal God's love in the most moving way?

Quite often we do in fact not live up to the life to which God has called us. Instead of being "dead to sin and alive to God" (Rom 6:11), we neglect or even break our baptismal commitment. God does not abandon the ungrateful sinner, but calls him back to repentance. After sin, repentance is the only way to restore again God's friendship.

1. The meaning of repentance

In order to understand the true meaning of repentance we must consider it under various aspects. There is the *basic initial commitment* by which we commit ourselves to break with sin and Satan, and to serve God as His beloved children (baptismal vows). We commit ourselves to a new life in Christ. This initial commitment does not only mean a break with sin, but it includes a commitment to the ongoing process of ever more perfect transformation into Christ. In this sense we must find repentance even in the life of a Christian who has avoided any deliberate sin after baptism. Since children could not commit themselves in the moment of baptism—it is the aim of catechesis for children to make them aware of God's life and love which was given to them before they even understood it, and to make them ever more ready for their later personal commitment of filial friendship to God.

But here we speak of *repentance for sins committed after baptism.* Personal sin always means our personal "no" to God: the "no" of minimizing and neglecting Him (venial sin) or the "no" of breaking with Him (mortal sin). Repentance means changing this "no" into a new "yes." We cannot repent without God's help (actual grace). But God's grace does not force us, it leaves us free. In true repentance after sin we can *distinguish three elements.* The most basic element consists in the new *acknowledgement of God's authority* ("Yes, you are the Lord. I am ready to obey"). But it also means that we *acknowledge God's justice* and admit that we did wrong and, therefore, deserve to be punished. This is difficult for our pride, but indispensable for true repentance after personal sin. Although we deserve punishment after sin, we also know that God is always ready to forgive—and to forgive fully—provided that we *appeal to His mercy* and ask His forgiveness. Without this trustful appeal to His mercy, no sin can be forgiven. Note e.g., Judas' useless "contrition." Mere fear of Hell, even in connection with confession does not bring forgiveness of sins. The personal "no" to God, must be retracted by a new and sincere personal "yes."

From all of this it is obvious that true repentance means a *change of heart and mind* after sin. The sinner must sincerely disapprove what he approved in the moment of sin. True repentance can only be found in the "heart," never just in the mouth. Any emphasis upon the *formula of contrition* is dangerous and harmful.

True repentance must prove itself in the change of our life. The *"works of repentance"* are above all the new way of life according to our change of mind. This is *indispensable.* If our repentance is sincere and deep, it will also make us ready to take upon ourselves additional hardships, like fasting, in order to prove the sorrow for our sins. We punish ourselves in order to serve God better in the future. Like any salutary punishment inflicted by others is intended as an aid to help the delinquent realize the malice of his action and to strengthen his decision not to repeat his wrong-doing again, so self-inflicted salutary penance is meant to manifest and to foster our interior change and to protect ourselves from falling back into the same fault again. The more all this is motivated by true love, the more our penance is truly Christian.

2. The sacrament of penance

After personal sin—venial or mortal—there is absolutely no way to be forgiven other than personal repentance. Nobody else, not even our Savior with his death on the cross, can substitute for this personal obligation of the sinner. The sacrament of repentance was not instituted to replace personal repentance but to promote and consecrate it.

a) Why Christ instituted the sacrament of repentance

The sacrament of repentance is the paschal gift of Our Lord. In this sacrament we meet Christ as the Good Shepherd, as the "friend of the sinners," who in the name of his Father forgives our sins and assures us of God's forgiveness. It has been instituted—primarily—for the reconciliation of Christians who have committed mortal sins, in order to help them find their way back to God and find again true peace and joy. Especially after serious sins there is a special need of:

1) *The consoling assurance* of God's certain and full forgiveness.
2) Accepting God's forgiveness as His *free and undeserved gift.* Forgiveness is by no means something the sinner can claim as something "due" to him and his own efforts of reparation. God surely forgives whenever man sincerely repents. But the sinner must accept it as the gift of undeserved mercy and must humbly accept the conditions under which God wants to forgive. By accepting these conditions he proves the sincerity of his new "yes" to God.
3) *A clear reminder of the necessity of repentance.* Without the help of the sacrament countless people would in fact just "forget" to repent.
4) *A renewal of the faith in Christ* as the only Savior. By making the sacrament of penance obligatory for the sinner after serious sin, God lets us realize (understand in an experiential way) that after sin there is only one way back to God: Christ our Savior whom we meet in the sacrament.
5) *A clear expression of the social aspect* of sin and repentance. The Church is by its very nature the community of God's obedient children. Our solemn commitment to break with sin and to serve God faithfully is the essential

condition for being accepted into the Church. Any serious sin means *a break of this commitment,* and an act against the very aim of the Church. It is, therefore, most meaningful that God, after mortal sin, demands as a condition of His forgiveness reconciliation with the Church through this sacrament.

b) *How to receive the sacrament of repentance as we should:*

In order to receive the sacrament well two conditions are essential:
1) True and sincere repentance for the sins which have been committed. In order to make us aware of these sins we examine our conscience. But it is much more important that we *truly repent,* that in the presence of God we humbly admit our fault, regret it and ask God's forgiveness for it.
2) Personal encounter with Christ in our sincere confession and the reception of his absolution. We meet and acknowledge Christ in his visible priest. Our main attention in confession must be concerned with Christ, however, and not with his visible representative. We speak to Christ, we consider *absolution* as his saving act.

AIDS FOR DISCUSSION AND ASSIMILATION

1. *How is the spirit of repentance a basic attitude of the Christian life?*
2. *What are the three constitutive elements of repentance after sin?*
3. *What is the value and right use of the formula of contrition?*
4. *What is meant by the "works of repentance"? Are they necessary?*
5. *Why did Christ institute the sacrament of penance?*
6. *What are the main conditions for receiving this sacrament well?*

31

The "Social" Sacraments: Orders and Matrimony

Is the universal priesthood of the laity real priesthood? Does it make hierarchical priesthood superfluous or less significant? How does one complement the other? What did Vatican II stress most especially with regard to family life?

All sacraments have an important social dimension. Through them, Christ intends not only to sanctify individual men, but "to build up the body of Christ" (CL, n. 59). Yet among all sacraments, two sacraments stand out for their social function: holy orders and matrimony. For both consecrate the recipient for a special important service within the community. Nobody receives these two sacraments for himself, but he does so for others.

1. Holy Orders

Through baptism and confirmation all Christians participate in the priesthood of Christ. They are a "chosen people, a royal priesthood, a holy nation, a purchased people" (1 Pt 2:9). Christ, the High Priest not only offers for them, but with them. This *universal priesthood* of all faithful does in no way exclude a special *hierarchical priesthood,* by which Christ calls and consecrates some of his members to a special participation in his priesthood and gives them special powers for their priestly work within the Church. This is, in fact, how Christ does it in his Church, through the sacramental sign—the imposition of hands by the Bishop. But this transfer of Christ's powers does not make the ordained priest a priest of his own; it makes him only an assistant and instrument of Christ, the High Priest. It is always Christ himself who acts out our salvation in the sacraments, although in collaboration with his visible ordained priest (remember the comparison with the dentist).

All greatness and dignity of the ordained priest consists of this, his close collaboration with Christ. His special privilege consists in his special duty of service, which he owes to the Church. The main *qualifications* for priesthood, therefore, are a deep personal dedication to the person of Christ and the spirit of selfless service.

In presenting the Orders, we must be careful that we never cover up the High Priest by his visible priest, and that we never minimize the universal priesthood of all the faithful.

2. Matrimony

Matrimony consecrates the Christian spouses to a stable (unbreakable) and exclusive union of conjugal love. This union of love receives its special dignity and holiness from its *participation in the mystery of Christ.* It sacramentally (a sign which realizes what it means) expresses the unbreakable and exclusive union of love between Christ and his Church (Eph 5:32).

The sacrament of matrimony consists not just in the valid celebration of the marriage settlement before the priest, but rather in the *life of love* which starts by this celebration. It is not the matrimonial contract itself, but the life of conjugal love according to this contract, which is the sacramental expression of Christ's perennial love for his Church.

Consequently, it is in their life of conjugal love that the husband and wife meet sacramentally Christ himself. In the married life of Christians everything must be understood and evaluated in the light of their "consecrated" love. As authentic love it must be more concerned to give than to receive, and as conjugal love it must, on principle, keep itself open to new life, according to God's plan of creation. Conjugal love, therefore, as the Council insists, must be harmonized with respect for life. "The Church issues the reminder that a true contradiction cannot exist between the divine laws pertaining to the transmission of life and those pertaining to the fostering of authentic conjugal love" (CMW, n. 51). In a case of an apparent conflict married Christians must sincerely try to inform their conscience correctly and to solve this conflict. True Christians are aware of their serious obligation to make their important decisions in a truly Christian way. In case of practically unsoluable conflict preference is to be given to conjugal love.

Because of the extreme importance of a healthy family life for human society and for the Kingdom of God, special care must be given to good religious instruction on God's plan for man and his life within a Christian family. This necessarily means solid *sex instruction.* According to Vatican II this instruction must be timely, positive and prudent. It also must be clear and comprehensive. Even more important than solid sex instruction—which is definitely necessary—is the early formation of the *necessary attitudes* which are indispensable for any happy family life: mutual respect, self-giving love, sense of responsibility and self-control.

AIDS FOR DISCUSSION AND ASSIMILATION

1. *Why do we call holy orders and matrimony the "social" sacraments?*
2. *What does universal priesthood of the laity and hierarchical priesthood of the ordained priest mean?*
3. *In what does the special dignity and privilege of the ordained priest consist?*
4. *What is the meaning of the sacrament of matrimony?*
5. *What are the main qualities of good sex instruction?*
6. *What are the main attitudes needed for happy family life?*

Following the Second Vatican Council, the religion teacher should show that marriage is the basis of family life. Special attention should be given to the unity and unbreakable quality of matrimony, as decreed by God. The purposes of marriage should be explained in accord with the teachings of the Second Vatican Council (Basic Teaching for Catholic Religious Education, n.13).

32

Preparing for the Coming of Christ

Can the sacrament of the sick or any other sacrament, at least in some exceptional cases, substitute for the lack of true repentance? What do we know about purgatory? What is its place in God's plan of salvation?

Already here on earth we are united with Our Lord the God-Man, he lives in us and we in him. We meet him in a special way in all his sacraments. We all will meet him, face-to-face—being fully aware of his presence—when we shall meet him in the moment of our death, and at the end of time when he comes again in glory to judge the living and the dead. Here we speak of preparing ourselves for his coming in the hour of our death.

1. The sacrament of the sick: The gift of God's healing love

In the same way as confirmation is closely related to baptism and complements it, the anointing of the sick is closely related to the sacrament of penance and must be seen as its complement. According to the Bible death and sickness, as we find and experience them in this our world, are the consequences of sin; they remind us of sin. God's forgiving and healing love comprises also the bodily and temporal consequences of sin. It is in this perspective we have to see Christ's loving concern for the sick which all gospels render prominent. In the anointing of the sick, Christ continues his care for the sick. There he meets us in our bodily sickness, in order to console and to comfort us. He helps us to see and accept sickness in a truly Christian way, as a gift of God: it should free us from attachment to this world and remind us of the shortness and frailty of human life.

2. The sacraments of the dying

When we present the sacrament of the sick, we speak rightly—with James 5:14f—first about its consoling, enlightening and strengthening effects in the times of bodily sickness. But it has still another important function: to help us see and accept life and death in a Christian way and to prepare us, together with the other sacraments of the dying, for our final union with Christ. With the help of these sacraments—of course, in connection with a Christian life—the Christian should be prepared to meet Christ at the moment of his death without needing further purification (purgatory). It is our sacramental preparation for our entrance into the heavenly wedding feast.

The faithful need to be often reminded that the sacraments of the dying are in *no way intended by God as a magical substitute* for a Christian life. This is of special importance with regard to the sacrament of the sick. It cannot bring any forgiveness of sin if the person who receives it has not truly repented of his sins. In case of an accident, the priest can definitely give the sacrament, supposing the right disposition of the unconscious person. But it remains an empty ceremony, if the sinner has not sincerely repented.

The sacraments of the dying mean our last sacramental meeting with Christ here on earth. As sacramental meetings, they suppose the commitment of faith and repentance; they prepare us for an even greater and lasting meeting with Christ.

3. Purgatory—a state of final purification

The doctrine on purgatory is best presented in connection with the sacraments of the dying. It is the state of final purification for those who died in the grace of God without being sufficiently prepared for their final union with God. They died without perfect repentance of their sins and without a deep desire for union with God forever. Purgatory helps them to perfect repentance and a consuming desire for union with God.

We do not know anything about the duration or the type of purification in purgatory other than that it is painful. Purgatory is not the antechamber of hell ("almost like hell, only shorter"), but the *antechamber of heaven.* In hell the enemies of God suffer, but in purgatory the friends of God suffer with patience, hope and love.

AIDS FOR DISCUSSION AND ASSIMILATION

1. *Why did Christ institute the sacrament of the sick?*
2. *What are the sacraments of the dying?*
3. *What is the best preparation for a good death?*
4. *What is meant by purgatory? Is it closer to heaven or to hell?*

> The importance of old age is still not sufficiently recognized in the pastoral ministry.
>
> In our times the number of the aged is increasing more and more. The aged are often neglected by contemporary society, however, and this fact must be carefully noted for its relevance to pastoral activity.
>
> As a matter of fact, the aged can contribute no small benefit to the community both by their work, which is not always justly appreciated, and by the witness that flows from their experience.
>
> Moreover, there is a duty in justice to help the aged by a catechesis that has reference to death, which biologically is near at hand, and socially is to some extent already present, since almost nothing is expected any more from their activity. . . .
>
> Unquestionably, it would be a serious loss to the Church if the great number of the aged who have been baptized were not to show that their faith shines with a brighter light when death approaches (General Catechetical Directory, n. 95).

33

The Second Coming of Christ

What would you consider the two most significant moments in the Christian life? Would you consider longing for the second coming of Christ a basic Christian attitude we have to communicate in authentic Christian formation? Do Christians of today, like the early Christian, really long for the Second Coming of Christ? Why not?

Christ came first into the world in his Incarnation. Sent by his heavenly Father, he came as Savior to call us to the Kingdom of God, to make us children of God. In all the sacraments he continues his first coming as Savior. When our time of testing is over—for each of us in the hour of death, and for all mankind at the last judgment—he will come again.

1. The purpose of his second coming

When he returns, he again will come *as Christ,* sent by his heavenly Father, manifesting the love of the Father. Further, he will come *as Savior,* but with a quite different task. In his Incarnation and in his sacraments he comes in order to call, to challenge, to plant and to cultivate—by his first coming we have been called to salvation, we have been put on the way of salvation, we have been helped to understand to accept freely the gift of God. Then he will come to bring in the heavenly harvest, to consummate salvation. Then the time of repentance will be over, those who repented and accepted God's love will receive from Christ and in their union with Christ the fruit of their repentance. Salvation will be finally accomplished in them. But those who finally rejected God's love, will remain finally frustrated. It is Christ who will decide who is worthy of being taken into his Kingdom of Glory. He comes *as judge.* Then nothing can be changed anymore; all must be changed and prepared now. With the abundant grace of God it is completely up to us, how we want to meet him then. Nobody has to fear anything from his judgment, who lives now a life of love and trust in his mercy.

Good catechesis *avoids fantastic descriptions* of the second coming of Christ, but does everything possible to build up a deep faith and desire for his second coming. Our life with Christ now must be seen in the light of his second coming. The true Christian is looking forward to it, not with fear, but with loving hope. "Look up and raise your heads, because your redemption is drawing near" (Lk 21:28). "He who testifies to these things says, 'Surely I am coming soon.' Amen. Come, Lord Jesus." (Rev. 22:20).

2. Meeting Christ in the hour of death

The certainty of death forces us to think of the meaning of our short lives. The unique irreparable value of this one life given to us now. The uncertainty of the hour of death helps us to keep ourselves always prepared. *Death* means for sinner and saint alike the absolute end of repentance, the end of our test. For the followers of the rebellious Adam death means the end of life and the beginning of everlasting death. For the followers of the obedient second Adam death means the end of our continuous dying to ourselves and the beginning of everlasting life. It depends upon us to make death a final success or a final collapse. Christian death means our decisive participation in the passover of Christ from complete submission unto God to the glory of resurrection. In the hour of death we meet Christ. This is the *particular judgment.*

3. Meeting Christ when he comes in glory

Although our eternal lot will be decided in the hour of our death, the Lord's coming in glory at the end of time contain very basic truths which we must present often and well to the faithful, avoiding fantastic descriptions.

a) *The final triumph of Christ.* The "day of the Lord." Then the Father will glorify His Son before the whole world, before his enemies. We do not know in any detail how this will happen. The imagery of the Bible does not want to reveal concrete details but wants to underline the basic truth of

Christ's final victory over all the powers of darkness, in undeniable evidence and unspeakable glory.

b) *The resurrection of the dead.* Christ will call us to share in the glories of his resurrection. This includes a *new bodily existence,* truly human, but essentially different from the manner of life we experience now. We cannot describe it. We must avoid all the useless questions we cannot in any way answer now. What we have to stress is the deep meaning of this article of faith: "We await a Savior, the Lord Jesus Christ, who will change our lowly body to be like his glorious body; by the power which enables him even to subject all things to him" (Phil 3:21). This will be our participation in the Paschal Mystery, even with the bodily aspect of our human existence.

c) *The general judgment.* Again we do not know any details of how it will be done. But its meaning is clear: Through Christ it will come to a complete and splendid *manifestation of God's plan of salvation* in all its details, showing how man from his very origins until the "day of the Lord" has responded to God's love. It will be a grandiose manifestation and justification of God's power, wisdom and love. Then the way of God's providence, now so often inscrutable, will be plain. Then the *community aspect* in God's plan of salvation will be shown in full evidence, how Christ is the center of the whole, how "all things have been created through and unto him, and he is before all creatures, and in him all things hold together" (Col 1:18).

AIDS FOR DISCUSSION AND ASSIMILATION

1. *Compare the first coming of Christ and its aim with his second coming and its aim.*
2. *What does it mean to say that Our Lord will come again as Christ, Savior and Judge?*
3. *What is the meaning of death?*
4. *What is the meaning of the resurrection of the dead?*

34

The Final Act in the Drama of God's Love for Man

How does the life in this world relate to the life to come? Is it only a time of ruthless test and preparation without meaning and value in itself, or is it intended by God also as a foretaste and anticipation of the final gift of His love? What follows from the answer to the preceding question for an authentic Christian attitude to our life on earth?

From the last judgment Christ will lead his brethren to enjoy eternal life in the Kingdom of his Father. Everything until then is only preparatory. We are not allowed to minimize our task and God's many gifts in this transitory life, but the final gift of God's love will surpass by far everything we have experienced on our way, although it will be in line with our life of now and will be its final consummation. Here we can only mention some basic principles for a good catechesis on this final manifestation of God's love.

1. Behold the climax in the story of God's love

It is not only the final (end) act in the great drama, but its very climax. All until then was preparation, and therefore it must be understood as the way up to this final goal. The way must be judged in the light of the goal. Under this aspect this final chapter is the most important of all: It shows God's love at its fullest.

By this we do not want to say, that in presenting God's message we should spend much time on this final chapter. What really counts is that all the rest is continuously shown as the way up to this final conclusion. In this chapter we have to avoid carefully any fantastic descriptions of Heaven, etc.

2. Godcentered presentation

Like any other chapter this one too—and even more than the others—must be presented in a truly God-centered way. Heaven means for us Christians not a particular place but the state of our final and perfect *union with God.* Our perfect sharing in His life, our final participation in the heritage of the Son (Rm 8:17). Heaven means for us essentially more than a mere "vision" of God; it is rather the unspeakable joy which results from our perfect and inseparable union with Him in love.

Heaven cannot be presented well by risky descriptions. We have to work with comparisons as Christ did. We must make clear that this final gift of God's will surpass by far all our joyful experiences here on earth. We must now believe in God's final love. All that God has done until now justifies our blind faith in His final love as something much greater than we can now experience and understand. "Blessed are those who have not seen and yet believe" (Jo 20:29). "No eye has seen, nor ear heard, nor the heart of man conceived, what God has prepared for those who love him" (1 Co 2:9).

The right and deep desire of final union with God can only be developed in a *life of prayerful union with God* here on earth, in the prayer experience of deep and sincere love of God. Whoever truly loves God will surely desire Heaven in the right way.

3. Heaven means fulfillment, means our final realization in Christ

Heavenly joy on the one hand surpasses by far all joyful experiences here on earth, but on the other hand it will be definitely and *perfectly human* (Comparison with an apple tree that tends to produce perfect apples and not books.) Avoid, therefore, any presentation of an "angelic" heaven. In heaven, man, as God had planned him in His love, will be actualized. But this man according to God's plan is fully oriented to God; through Christ, he is perfectly integrated into the heavenly community of the whole Christ. It will be, in fact, our conscious joyous participation in the *realization of the whole Christ,* head and members. And this will mean the perfect communication of the *Holy Spirit.* He makes us forever perfectly one with Christ and with all his members, and lets us pray forever: ABBA, FATHER!

AIDS FOR DISCUSSION AND ASSIMILATION

1. *Why is this final chapter of special importance?*
2. *What does Godcentered presentation of heaven mean?*
3. *What is the best means to let deep holy desire of heaven grow?*
4. *In what sense does heaven mean our final realization in Christ?*

> Listen! I stand at the door and knock; if anyone hears my voice and opens the door, I will come into his house and eat with him, and he will eat with me. To those who win the victory I will give the right to sit by me on my throne, just as I have been victorious, and now sit by my Father on his throne (Rev 3:20f).

Bibliography

Durwell, Francois Xavier, C.SS.R. *The Resurrection. A Biblical Study*. New York: Sheed and Ward, 1960.

Evely, Louis. *Credo*. Notre Dame: Fides, 1967.

Farrel, Melvin L., S.S. *Theology for Parents and Teachers.* Milwaukee: Hi-Time Publications, 1972.

Fransen, Piet, S.J. *The New Life of Grace.* New York: Desclee, 1969.

Grasso, Domenico, S.J. *Proclaiming God's Message.* Notre Dame: Notre University Press, 1965.

Hitz, Paul, C.SS.R. *To Preach the Gospel.* New York: Sheed and Ward, 1963.

Hofinger, Johannes, S.J. and Francis Buckley, S.J. *The Good News and Its Proclamation.* Notre Dame: Notre Dame University Press, 1968.

Jungmann, Josef, S.J. *The Good News, Yesterday and Today.* New York: Sadlier, 1962.

Liegé, P.A., O.P. *What Is Christian Life?* New York: Hawthorn Books, 1961.

Moran, Gabriel, F.S.C. *Theology of Revelation.* New York: Herder and Herder, 1966.

Nebreda, Alfonso, S.J., *Kerygma in Crisis?* Chicago: Loyola University Press, 1965.

Rahner, Hugo, S.J. *Theology of Proclamation.* New York: Herder and Herder, 1968.

Ratzinger, Josef, *Introduction into Christianity.* New York: Herder and Herder, 1970.

Scheeben, Matthias Josef, *The Mysteries of Christianity.* St. Louis: Herder, 1946.

Schillebeeck, Edward, O.P. *Christ, The Sacrament of the Encounter with God.* New York: Sheed and Ward, 1963.

Van Caster, Marcel, S.J. *Themes of Catechesis.* New York: Herder and Herder, 1965.

Varillon, Francois, *Announcing Christ.* Westminster: Newman, 1964.

Wilhelm, A. *Christ Among Us.* Revised edition. Paramus, N.Y.: Newman Press, 1973.

A New Catechism. Catholic Faith for Adults. New York: Herder and Herder, 1967.

Basic Teachings for Catholic Religious Education. National Conference of Catholic Bishops. Washington: Catholic Conference, 1973.

General Catechetical Directory. Issued by the Sacred Congregation of the Clergy. Washington: Catholic Conference, 1971.

Index